Mastering
the
Tarot

Mastering the Tarot

An Advanced Personal Teaching Guide

Juliet Sharman-Burke

St. Martin's Griffin
New York

To Sarah, who was there at the beginning,
with love

Library of Congress Cataloging-in-Publication Data available on request

ISBN 0-312-26762-2

First St. Martin's Griffin Edition 2000

10 9 8 7 6 5 4 3 2 1

AN EDDISON • SADD EDITION

Edited, designed and produced by
Eddison Sadd Editions Limited
St Chad's House
148 King's Cross Road
London, WC1X 9DH

Phototypeset in Iowan Old Style BT and Calligraph 421 BT using
QuarkXPress on Apple Macintosh
Origination by Pixel Graphics, Singapore
Printed by Kyodo Printing Co., Singapore

CONTENTS

Introduction

This book is intended as a companion to *Understanding the Tarot*, in which I introduced the symbolic and divinatory meanings of the seventy-eight tarot cards, using a number of different tarot decks. The tarot has many layers of meaning and its study is an endlessly fascinating pursuit. In this volume, I offer an understanding of the deeper levels of the symbolism by deciphering the more obscure aspects and provide some practical exercises that will heighten your imagination and intuition when reading the cards. Once again – with the kind permission of my students – I have reproduced some of the conversations that have taken place during teaching sessions, as students' questions have often raised important issues. My aim is to provide a teaching platform that will enable you to further your mastery of the tarot and to enjoy it as much as I do.

This book sets out to find a modern application for an ancient system. As detailed factual information on the specific uses for which the tarot was intended does not exist, this process involves a certain amount of divination and speculation. In unravelling the many layers of symbolic meaning contained in the cards, I draw on the rich and varied sources of religious and spiritual beliefs and mythologies that may have contributed to the existence of the tarot. And I draw parallels between the cards of the Major Arcana and the alchemical process of spiritual and psychological transformation.

The Emergence of the Cards

The tarot made its first documented appearance in Western Europe in the early fifteenth century. Although we still do not know who designed the images and for what purpose, we can draw some possible conclusions by studying the period in history from which the cards first emerged.

The eleventh, twelfth and thirteenth centuries saw a huge revival of learning in Western Europe. The opening of trade routes to the East meant that new concepts and beliefs flowed into Europe, stimulating great interest and curiosity. Ideas from the East filtered through

Italy to France, and on to Flanders and the north-west of Germany. At the same time the Norman conquest of England enabled Celtic beliefs, such as the Grail legends, to enter Europe through the courts of northern France. As a result, European civilization became rich with material from many diverse sources, fuelling a keen appetite for spiritual and psychological growth, which was not satisfied by the established Church.

During the twelfth century, Gnosticism became increasingly popular. The term 'Gnostic' derives from the Greek *gnosis*, meaning knowledge, and Gnosticism combined Greek philosophy and Hebrew cabbalistic beliefs with Indian, Chaldean, Persian and Egyptian magical doctrines.[1] Gnostic religious sects, such as the Waldenses, Cathars, Albigenses and Bogomils, enjoyed considerable success before they were perceived as a threat to the established Church in the middle of the thirteenth century, after which they were systematically stamped out.

The Influence of the Cathars

The Cathars, a dualistic sect, believed that the universe was split into two by opposing powers. They saw the physical world as evil, a creation of the devil, who they believed to be the God of the Old Testament. Christ was the saviour sent to show how man could be freed from his bond with the material world, reveal the true nature of the dark Old Testament God and become one with the light. They believed the human spirit was the divine spark of God trapped in the material world and furthermore they believed that humans suffered, not because of original sin but rather because a primeval tragedy occurred, which was beyond their control. Consequently, the redemption of humans would also be the redemption of God, and when the evil world was defeated, the part of God that was trapped in matter would also be released, enabling it to return to its source.[2]

The beliefs of the Cathars could be understood as mirrored in the cards of the Major Arcana. Man's spirit, divine yet trapped in human form and ignorant of its great potential, is represented by The Fool. A divine messenger (The Magician) shows people how to master the material world. The structures of the material world must be understood and complied with (The High Priestess, The Empress, The

Emperor and The Hierophant), and the trials and challenges of daily life surmounted (The Lovers and The Chariot, Justice, Temperance and Strength). When The Fool has reached maturity (The Hermit), he is in a position to take the inner journey (The Wheel of Fortune), which involves the sacrifice of the conscious ego (The Hanged Man), the loss of the lower self (Death) and the battle with evil forces (The Devil). This battle results in the release from earthly shackles (The Tower) and allows passage through the heavenly spheres (The Star, The Moon and The Sun). At the end of this journey there follows the mystical rebirth (Judgement) and final, triumphant merging with the universe (The World).

Classical Influences

The Italian Renaissance stimulated a revival of interest in classical Greece. The multiplicity of Greek gods offered a more complex and perhaps more interesting pattern of the universe than the somewhat static world of the Christian Trinity, which was exclusively male. And the Greek myths provided the artists who created the early Renaissance tarot decks with a rich source of symbolic imagery.

After the sacking of Constantinople by the Turks in 1453, a great many Greek manuscripts, particularly the writings of Plato and the Neoplatonists and the Hermetic philosophies of Alexandra and the Middle East, found their way into Western Europe. These manuscripts arrived in Florence at a time when the city's rulers were open to new ideas, and a fresh spirit of learning was encouraged by the recently invented printing press.[3]

The Neoplatonic–Hermetic movement offered the view that humankind was a microcosm of the greater universe and that self- and soul-knowledge were the only true religious paths through which one could be reconnected with one's divine origins. The Renaissance vision declared that man was a 'miracle', challenging previously held Christian beliefs that man was a poor sinner who could only hope to know God through the intermediary of the Church.

In the face of this competition, the established Church began to feel threatened and acted violently to quash the new vision and retain its political and spiritual stronghold. Paradoxically, however, Gnostic lore, astrology and alchemy survived the attempts of the Holy

Inquisitions to stamp them out because the documents that contained detailed accounts of their beliefs and teachings were preserved within the Church itself, in the monasteries – places of learning where the older doctrines were studied as a matter of course. The monastic libraries often possessed forbidden copies of such ancient spell-books because it was believed that 'in order to counter Satan's wiles, one must know the type of creature one is dealing with'.[4]

Using Images for Meditation

The Ancient Greeks used images as part of a memory system in which they associated information they wanted to remember with key images, so that later they had only to look at the image to recall the 'linked' information. They also used to meditate upon images as a way of approaching the gods. The images of Greek gods, such as those that appear on the early Renaissance tarot decks, were understood to be symbols of the great laws at work through the whole of creation. By meditating upon these images it was hoped that 'memory' of the divine world of the soul would be restored. This would, in turn, raise the individual consciousness from its entrapment in the mundane or material world and connect the soul with its source.[5]

In the Middle Ages, pictures were an important educational tool as few people could read. Books were difficult to produce in large numbers as they had to be produced singly, by hand. So series of paintings were commissioned for public places where large numbers of people could be instructed and educated at once. Frescoes illustrating biblical stories, such as Adam and Eve's expulsion from paradise, Noah's Ark and Jacob's many-coloured coat, were created for this purpose, together with scenes from the New Testament of the birth, death and resurrection of Christ. The great artist of the early Italian Renaissance, Giotto, painted such frescoes in the Arena Chapel, Padua, and some historians have pointed out that the images Giotto uses, of the virtues Justice, Temperance and so forth, are similar to those depicted on the cards of the Major Arcana.

The Church encouraged meditation using religious imagery to deepen spiritual understanding. The pictorial decorations in churches of the Middle Ages were all designed to improve the congregation's understanding of the mysteries of Christ's life and death. Using pictures for meditation was also carried out in monasteries. An example of such imagery can still be seen in the monastery of St Marco in Florence, where Fra. Angelico, a renowned Italian artist and monk, painted a scene from the life of Christ in each monastic cell. The intention was that the monk who inhabited that cell should meditate intensely on the image for hours at a time, entering deeply into whichever aspect of Christ's life was depicted. By engaging so totally with the image, the monk was expected to reach a true understanding of the mysteries of Christ's life, death and resurrection.

The Renaissance movement adopted a similar practice of meditation, using a series of magical, symbolic images in order to reach higher levels of consciousness and to gain insights into the divine world. It seems quite possible that the main purpose of the tarot was also the illumination of consciousness. The tarot uses complex, sometimes contradictory, symbolic images to communicate several different meanings through the imagination, feeling and intuition. The tarot images speak to the conscious and the unconscious mind at the same time. Some of these images feel comforting, others threatening, although we may not always be aware of why this is. And the more you work with, or meditate upon, the imagery on the cards, the better you become at deciphering its meanings.

Connections with Alchemy

There are also obvious parallels between the tarot and the medieval alchemist, whose life's work was dedicated to the production of gold from base material. Alchemical texts state over and over again that the true purpose of the great work was the process of illumination and transformation of the conscious mind, although the common myth pers   hat alchemists were lunatics trying to get rich by turning lead into gold. This is not dissimilar to the popular misconception that the tarot is a mere 'fortune-telling device'.

Correlations can be made between the alchemical work and The Fool's journey through the twenty-two cards of the Major Arcana. The base material (lead) could be seen as The Fool himself, who must combine with the other cards to reach completion in the final card, The World (gold). The base material, according to the alchemist, was available everywhere cheaply and yet was something very difficult to find. It was said to contain within it different disharmonious energies – intellectual, imaginative and emotional – symbolized by the seven ancient planets – the Sun, the Moon, Mercury, Venus, Mars, Jupiter and Saturn. Together these energies contained spiritual potential (or alchemical gold) but it required the alchemist to bring harmony to the warring elements in order to release that potential. In the same way we (The Fool) all have spiritual potential but few of us are prepared to engage in the painstaking task of fulfilling it.

The alchemist (The Magician) had first to separate the base material (composed of the four astrological elements – Earth, Water, Fire and Air) into the principles of passive female (Philosophic Mercury to be refined into silver or The Moon) and active male (Philosophic Sulphur to be refined into gold or The Sun). Silver and gold then had to be conjoined to produce a harmonious whole by adding the catalyst salt (represented by the god Mercury). The various tasks were performed according to the astrological year: spring – new birth, summer – abundance, autumn – decay, winter – death.

Alchemists held that the divine faculty possessed by man was his imagination, and their theory seems to have been that if the imagination was sufficiently well disciplined and concentrated it would produce amazing results. The alchemical work involved a combination of meditation and concentration on the images that emerged as a result of the material processes. Using similar imaginative techniques with the tarot can provide a spread with psychological richness. A person's life – both inner and outer – can be seen reflected in symbolic form by each of the Major cards.

The King and Queen's Progress

There is an alchemical story that can be equated with the Fool's progress through the Major Arcana. It is of a King (The Fool or the base material) who is born perfect and possesses the quality of perfection, yet for some mysterious reason has become sterile and his lands barren. The virile, conscious, active masculine principle (The Emperor, The Hierophant, The Sun) has been cut off from the fertile, unconscious female root (The High Priestess, The Empress, The Moon), resulting in drought and death. In order to save himself and his kingdom, the King (The Fool) must enter the underworld of

femaleness, or darkness, and perform a magical ceremony or sacred marriage to bring about a synthesis of these two warring elements (Temperance, The Lovers). He must descend into the darkness (The Hanged Man) and mate with the female principle, the Queen, sometimes called the virgin (The High Priestess), sometimes the mother (The Empress) and sometimes the hag (The Moon), each aspects of the multifaceted principle of femininity. The Queen is always related to the King in some way, which symbolizes that they are from the same root, so an incestuous union or marriage results. The sacred union, or *conjuntio*, is followed immediately by the death of the King (Death, The Devil, The Tower).

This stage of the alchemical process was known as the *nigredo*, or blackening, when it was hoped that the substance cooking in the alchemist's pot would turn black and stink. In order to find alchemical gold it was thought necessary for the male principle to be overwhelmed by the irrational part of the psyche – the female principle – otherwise known as the spirit of nature. The King dies as the Queen is impregnated. The next phase was the whitening, or *albedo*, when the Moon rules (The Star and The Moon) and the female principle has supremacy. Eventually the Queen gives birth, heralding the phase of the reddening, or *rubedo* (The Sun, Judgement), when the material cooking in the pot was expected to turn red. The final phase was the production of the elixir. When he reached this phase the alchemist was transformed simultaneously into Mercurius, an androgynous figure symbolizing the union of male and female, to make a perfect whole (The World). The product of the work might be the elixir of life, which could heal all ills, or the alchemical gold which, when combined with any other substance, would transform it into pure gold.

Links with the Mystery Plays

Another possible relation of the cards of the Major Arcana can be found in the Mystery plays, a supernatural drama or sacred history enacted before the followers of that cult or religion. The play begins with the birth of a semi-divine hero and continues with his life, loves, and successes and difficulties. Half-way through his life he meets with some crisis, perhaps the loss of a loved one or even his own death. This is followed by his perilous journey to the other world to face the spirits responsible, with whom he has to struggle. He returns victorious to the everyday world with the sought-after treasure, be it an object, a loved one or his own life regained. He is greeted with joy, for he has struggled with death and disaster, and triumphed.

There are records of the twenty-two cards of the Major Arcana (also known as Trumps) being used in Renaissance Italy in a game called Triumphs. This was also the name given to the tableaux that formed part of the Mystery Plays and processions.

The Major Arcana has also been connected with the greater Mysteries of Eleusis in Greece, which comprised four great religious festivals held in the spring and autumn over a period of two years. These were open to everyone and were extremely popular, sharing with early Christianity the notion of resurrection and afterlife. The first spring festival commemorated the abduction of Persephone by Hades; the following autumn festival solemnized the mourning of Demeter. The second spring festival celebrated the birth, life and violent death of Dionysus, culminating in Hades feeding Dionysus' heart, in the form of pomegranate seeds, to Persephone, who duly became pregnant and was established as an underworld deity for part of the year. The second autumn festival celebrated the trumphant rebirth of Dionysus as Iacchus, god of light. Further details concerning these Greek myths can be found in the text accompanying the cards of The Fool, The High Priestess and The Empress.

The Mystery cycle of the pagan initiate's triumphs came to be paralleled in Christianity with the birth of Jesus from semi-divine parentage, his progress through the material world toward death, descent into the underworld, triumphant resurrection and ascent into the heavens. Whether Orphic, Eleusinian, Mithraic or Christian, the theme is the same, and the procession of the twenty-two Major Arcana cards reflects a fusion of these cults, each image capturing some specific facet of human experience.[6]

REFERENCES   1. Paul Huson, *The Devil's Picturebook*
2. Alfred Douglas, *The Tarot*
3. Sharman-Burke, Greene, *The Mythic Tarot*
4. Paul Huson, *The Devil's Picturebook*
5. Sharman-Burke, Greene, *The Mythic Tarot*
6. Paul Huson, *The Devil's Picurebook*

CHAPTER ONE

THE MAJOR ARCANA

This chapter explores in detail the symbolism of the twenty-two cards of the Major Arcana. I have used a number of different decks to illustrate different aspects of each card. The oldest cards included are a reproduction of the fifteenth-century Visconti-Sforza deck. Swiss occultist and mason, Oswald Wirth, published his deck in 1889. The Universal Waite deck dates from 1910 and was drawn by Pamela Colman-Smith under the supervision of Arthur Edward Waite. This deck was a strong influence on the Morgan-Greer deck, which was designed in 1979. The other decks used – the Mythic Tarot, the Arthurian Tarot, the Renaissance Tarot

and the Medieval Scapini – are all products of the 1980s. The Medieval Scapini took its inspiration from the Middle Ages, and features the gold background, costumes and settings typical of that period. The Renaissance deck features images from classical mythology, and includes motifs that represent the four elements. The Mythic Tarot took its inspiration from the myths of Greek mythology, while the Arthurian deck drew on the magical tales of King Arthur.

Reference is made in discussing the cards to their historical associations with alchemy, astrology and mythology. The psychological significance of each card is also explained and divinatory meanings indicated. I have included some specially designed exercises for each card, involving meditation and visualization. These exercises will help increase your familiarity with each card as well as acting as a tool for self-discovery and understanding.

THE FOOL

The Visconti Sforza deck shows The Fool standing in stockinged feet, shabby and bedraggled. He has none of the external trappings that signify importance in the material and social world.

Most tarot commentators would agree that The Fool is one of the most important cards in the deck, not least because his image is so contradictory. On face value, he can be mistaken as light and frivolous, often depicted walking without apparent care towards the edge of a cliff. Yet, when we dig a little deeper, we uncover a highly ambivalent and complex nature to the unnumbered trump – the only one of the Major Arcana to have remained in our modern deck, as the Joker. Just like the Joker, The Fool belongs anywhere and can combine with any other card, adding life and energy. Marked with a '0', we can visualize him as the beginning of the zodiacal calendar, Aries, and as the first day of spring. This is a highly potent time: the start of a new cycle, the fertilized seed, the birth of a new year; and with each beginning anything and everything is possible. All is in potential and nothing has yet marred the overwhelming sense of opportunity that lies ahead. All this is true of The Fool in a positive sense when he appears in a spread.

The archetype of The Fool is a deep and highly significant one because he represents each one of us at every stage of life's journey. No matter how old or experienced we are, life continues to throw up new situations in which we find ourselves feeling vulnerable, at risk and uncertain. The image of The Fool, poised at the edge of a precipice, conjures up that moment of fear, excitement, dread and thrill that accompanies any new venture.

Humble Beginnings

The oldest image, in the Visconti Sforza deck (*above*), shows The Fool as a beggar. We might well dismiss this figure as someone with no status and no consequence. However, he carries a staff, which symbolizes that he is on a journey, and journeys go hand-in-hand with discoveries. If we think of the Mystery Plays discussed in the Introduction (*see page 13*), we may see echoes in this card of the Christian mystery, which starts with Jesus' humble birth in a stable, continues with his life as an ordinary carpenter and ends with his death and triumphant rebirth as the Prince of Peace. The Visconti Fool may thus symbolize that great power and victory are not always visible from the outside.

Just as all that glitters is not always gold, conversely, gold may be found inside the most unpromising exterior. The Fool may be equated with the alchemist's *Prima Materia* or Primal Matter, namely lead, which, when it undergoes a particular sequence of stages, eventually transforms into gold. Similarly, The Fool combines with different stages and phases of life's experience, as symbolized by each of the Major Arcana, and is changed and transformed. The work of the ancient alchemist involved a complex process during which opposites were combined and destroyed, separated, purified and reunited. By repeated separation and reunion, of letting go and gathering in, the work gradually and painstakingly continued through trial and error towards the vision of perfection. The Fool's journey through the Major Arcana follows a similar path.

The Fool in the Wirth Tarot is in a jester's costume. He is a medieval king's Fool, which means that he alone could tell truths to the king, something that no one else would dare attempt.

Overcoming Opposition

The Wirth deck (*right*) shows a strange figure in multi-coloured attire plodding on regardless of the fact that his left leg is being ravaged by a strange, cat-like creature, and oblivious to the crocodile, whose nose we can just see as it lurks waiting in the abyss. This image implies that the overwhelming impulse in The Fool to proceed on his expedition, despite all opposition, is stronger than the obstacles in his way.

le fou

Student *What does the crocodile signify?*

Juliet The crocodile may refer to the Egyptian myth of Isis and her son Horus, who were forced to hide in the swamps of the

Nile in fear of Horus' wicked uncle, Seth, who planned to murder his nephew as well as his brother. One of the forms Seth took was the crocodile (and it is possible that the legend of St George fighting the dragon was derived from images of Horus fighting Seth as a crocodile). Horus finally overpowered his evil relative and succeeded to the throne of his murdered father, Osiris. As a result, the living pharaoh of Egypt was regarded as Horus, the lord of sky and sun. The Fool in the tarot is linked to the child Horus, who, although he is heir to the throne, must first conquer the dark forces before he can succeed the dead king, who is represented by the fallen obelisk on the Wirth card. Images of Horus as a baby with his mother have probably influenced Christian iconography of the Virgin and child.

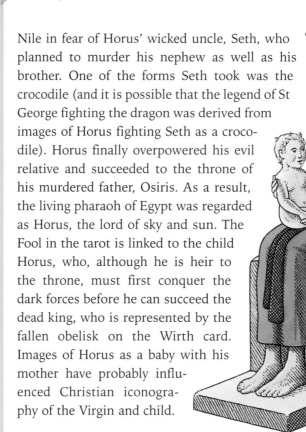

Keeping to the Path

The Arthurian Tarot (*left*) depicts The Fool as Parsifal, also known as Peredur, the Seeker of the Holy Grail of Arthurian myth. Parsifal's father was a fine and worthy knight of the Round Table but he died before his son was born. It was Parsifal's wish to become a knight too, although his mother did all she could to prevent him leaving. His mother finally agreed to let him go on condition that he dressed in fool's clothing, hoping this would attract such derision that he would return home, but Parsifal persevered in his quest in spite of the mockery. The tarot Fool offers this same message: we must follow our own path no matter who mocks us or calls our vision foolish. We must have the courage of our convictions no

o the seeker

matter how hard this might be at the time. Parsifal goes on to learn and understand the fine ideals that will make him a true knight.

Rebirth and Renewal

The Renaissance Tarot (*right*) portrays The Fool as the Greek Dionysus – the god of light and ecstasy – whose semi-divine birth, violent death and triumphant resurrection have parallels with the Christian story. Both Dionysus and Jesus had earthly mothers and divine fathers. Dionysus was dismembered and made whole again; his grapevine is pruned in the autumn in order to be renewed in spring. The Fool is depicted here in the costume of a sixteenth-century court jester. He carries a staff decorated with grapes and a skull, both suggesting Dionysian abandon and terror.

O·IL MATTO·THE FOOL·

The Renaissance Tarot shows lily-of-the-valley growing at Dionysus' feet. This calls to mind the advent of spring as well as simplicity and innocence.

• EXERCISE •

Sit or lie in a comfortable position and close your eyes. Clear your mind, take in a few deep breaths and imagine yourself as The Fool in the card, or in your own landscape. Stand at the edge of the precipice and be aware of your feelings. Note your own sense of excitement or fear, and try to be aware of what goes through your mind. Can you imagine the next stage – that leap over the edge? What happens? What awaits you? What do you land upon? Allow yourself to enter into the world of imagination and wander there for a while. On returning to the everyday world, make notes or record your experiences. Next, think of a situation that conjures up The Fool experience for you. This could be a time in which you needed to take a risk, perhaps fly in the face of the 'sensible' advice of others, metaphorically leaping in the dark. Consider carefully your own attitude to The Fool card, noting down the thoughts, feelings and associations that emerge spontaneously as you gaze at the image.

THE MAGICIAN

I·IL BAGATTO·THE MAGICIAN·8

A detail in the corner of the Renaissance card reveals a crane, the sacred bird of the Egyptian god Thoth, who was the inventor of language and scribe to the gods.

The Magician is The Fool's guide and helpmate on his journey towards inner understanding. As a guide and teacher, The Magician has many connections with the versatile, volatile Greek god Hermes, whose Egyptian name was Thoth and whose Roman name was Mercury. Thoth was honoured as a supreme teacher of many and various subjects, including astrology, astronomy, alchemy, chemistry and the medicinal powers of precious stones and plants.

Messenger of the Gods

Hermes was communicator, teacher and messenger of the Greek gods. Although seemingly 'lightweight' in comparison to the Olympians who ruled the sky or ocean, he actually exercised a great deal of influence on the everyday lives of humans. As the son of Zeus and the nymph Maia, he negotiated between the men and gods, and was the archetypal wheeler-dealer. He was the god of thieves and sharp practice as well as fanciful make-believe.

Hermes was also god of words. He promised his father Zeus he would not tells lies as long as he was not bound to tell the whole truth. On the morning of his birth he stole his brother Apollo's cattle and by the afternoon he had charmed a tortoise out of its shell to make a lyre, using cow gut for strings. This he swiftly offered in appeasement to Apollo, who was so enchanted he promptly forgave the theft and taught Hermes how to divine the future. Hermes was a master of manipulation, flattery and charm, turning every situation to his advantage. No dealings occurred on Olympus of which he was unaware, and hardly any in which he was not involved. He was implicated in almost every aspect of human life, from birth to death. His role as psychopomp involved guiding the souls of the dead to Hades, and he was among very few gods who could enter and leave the underworld unaffected.

Hermes' close links with all aspects of life, mortal and divine, is evidenced by the items on the Magician's table (*right*): the Wand, the Cup, the Sword and the Pentacle. The Pentacle represents commerce or material gain. Zeus made Hermes responsible for supervising the promotion of commerce and for organizing free passage for merchants and travellers on all the routes of the world in his role as patron to merchants. The Cup symbolizes love, both romantic and familial – Hermes frequently offered assistance in the complex love lives of the gods. The Sword represents war or conflict and in his role as Zeus' herald, Hermes was sometimes called upon to assist in battle. The Wand is a symbol of imagination, the quality that sets man apart from animals. Hermes is credited with having taught the gods to create fire by rubbing sticks together, and was thus involved in connecting all aspects of life: the mortal with the divine, the material with the spiritual.

THE MAGICIAN

The items on the Magician's table also connect with the four astrological elements of Fire, Water, Air and Earth, and represent the different directions life has to offer. In certain cultures it was customary to spread out a selection of articles in front of a young person in the belief that the one he or she selects will influence the course of his or her life. One could imagine that selecting the Cup would suggest love and relationships would be paramount in that person's life, while the Pentacles might indicate a desire for wealth would dominate. The Wand might suggest a wish to create, while the Sword could point to a desire to fight.

The Mythic Tarot shows The Magician as Hermes, god of crossroads, where travellers asked for his protection and blessing on their journeys.

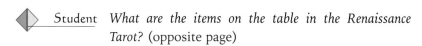

Student   *What are the items on the table in the Renaissance Tarot?* (opposite page)

Juliet   They are the basic forms that make up the world of man: the cube represents the material world; the sphere, the cycle of life; the pyramid, the three aspects of man: body, mind and spirit; and the polyhedron, which has twelve faces, the twelve signs of the zodiac. They stand on his three-legged stool, which symbolizes the three stages of man: youth, maturity and old age.

In his hand, Hermes (right) holds the caduceus, his wand of magic entwined with two snakes suggesting all opposites: good and evil, light and dark, male and female.

The Essential Catalyst

The god Hermes/Mercury is connected in alchemy with Salt, the essential ingredient required to bring about alchemical changes. The Philosophic Sulphur, or masculine energy, combines with Philosophic Mercury, the feminine, and they are separated and conjoined with the aid of Salt.

The first step is to identify the Primal Matter, the substance that contains all that is necessary to achieve perfection, but is in its chaotic, unrefined state. The Fool is equated with Primal Matter; he is full of potential, ideas, impulses and great energy but the energy is undirected and the ideas unfocussed. It is necessary to add a catalyst, Salt, to the unrefined substances to start the process of transformation. Psychologically, The Magician represents the spark of creative imagination needed to start the process of growth and change.

On the Universal Waite card, the Magician's outstretched arms point towards Heaven and Earth; he is connected and committed to both.

THE MAGICIAN.

The Magician in the Universal Waite deck (*left*) is dressed in red and white, colours that are repeated in the flowers surrounding him, representing the opposites of male and female, passion and purity. This can be seen as a reflection of the need to separate these out, as in the alchemical process, before joining them again to achieve perfection. The red roses may symbolize the Red King, who personifies gold, while the white lilies symbolize the White Queen, who represents silver. The Magician represents the Salt, the essential catalyst that first separates and then joins the two in perfect harmony. In a tarot reading, The Magician suggests that there is a spark of an idea, which must be acted upon to become manifest. The Red King and the White Queen could not produce the Alchemical Gold if it were not for the action of the Salt.

The Fairground Trickster

Many of the old decks, like the Medieval Scapini deck (*right*), show the Magician in the guise of a fairground conjurer performing a sleight-of-hand trick. In some decks he appears to be selling trinkets commonly found in markets and fairs, such as the little bottle purporting to contain the elixir of life, or at least a cure-all for any disease. We are tempted to believe the fantastic claims yet we are sceptical. The Magician offers an image of one who may be truly magical or merely accomplished at the art of deception, but who knows for sure? One can never tell whether he is leading you towards a magical treasure or simply down a dead-end track! When he appears in a reading, the Magician suggests that new opportunities are available, together with the energy to pursue them, but that the path is by no means clear.

The Scapini deck depicts The Magician wearing red with white trim, reflecting the opposites of male and female, solar and lunar. A red flower pushes through the stony ground, a symbol of inspiration bursting through uncertainty.

• EXERCISE •

Choose a colour that you feel best encapsulates the overall character of The Magician. It can be whichever colour you like, as long as you can use it as your personal signature for this card. Lie flat on your back and close your eyes. Breathe deeply and rhythmically. Now imagine that there are holes in the soles of your feet into which your chosen colour is pouring. Visualize your limbs being filled with the colour of The Magician. Note your feelings. Then allow the colour to slowly drain away, leaving your whole body relaxed. Imagine closing the holes in the your feet. Again, note your feelings.

You should feel very relaxed and ready for another meditation. Allow the images of the Cup, the Sword, the Wand and the Pentacle to drift one by one through your mind. Which symbol do you feel most drawn to at the moment? Why do you think this is? Follow the thought and examine the stage you are at personally at the moment. Make a note of your observations.

THE HIGH PRIESTESS

The Visconti deck shows a woman in brown monastic robes, wearing a headdress reminiscent of a papal crown over a white wimple. She holds a closed book, which indicates that there are answers to all questions, but that they are not easily available.

Essentially, The High Priestess is a card of mystery. Her name on the tarot has changed a few times over the centuries, one of her earliest names being The Papess or The Female Pope, while the Swiss 1JJ deck of the seventeenth century shows her as Juno, consort of Roman Jupiter. Court de Gebelin, an eighteenth-century tarot expert, changed it to The High Priestess when he 'discovered' what he believed to be a link between the tarot and ancient Egypt, and connected her with the goddess Isis. The High Priestess is now the name most commonly used name on modern tarot decks.

The Female Pope

The title of Papess or Female Pope is said by some to refer to the ancient legend of Pope Joan, which tells of a girl, Joan, who fell in love with a monk and disguised herself as a man so that she could follow him to Rome to be with him. When her lover died, she continued the pretence that she was a man and was in due course elected to the Papal Chair. This historically unfounded tale may have arisen from some of the heretical sects, like the Cathars, who, unusually for the times, permitted women to hold positions of authority. They believed that their founder, Guglielma of Bohemia, who died in 1281, would rise again in 1300 and begin a new age in which women would be popes. There was an Italian group in existence in the late thirteenth century called the Guglielmites. They elected a woman named Manfreda Visconti as pope. They believed her to be the incarnation of the Holy Spirit. However, she was burned as a heretic by the Church in 1300. Curiously, some hundred years later, an image appeared in a deck of cards commissioned by the Visconti family of a woman wearing what looks like the religious habit worn by the Guglielmites.

The Virgin or Maiden

The Female Pope as a card introduces another dimension of the feminine archetype, a darker, more spiritual and mysterious side, which is not simply 'Mother'.

In other old decks, The High Priestess appears under the title of Juno, the Roman name for Hera, heavenly sister and wife of Zeus and sister of Demeter, the Earth Mother. It seems, in this context, that she represents the celestial side of the Earth Mother. The whole archetype of the feminine is made up of the triple-faced goddess – the Virgin, the Mother and the Hag, and The High Priestess describes the first, youthful face.

◆ **Student** *Isn't The High Priestess also connected with the New Moon, the phase of promise before fulfilment?*

◆ **Juliet** Yes. As Virgin, she represents the first quarter, full of potential and energy, which works away quietly until it reaches fruition at the Full Moon – described by the Empress (*see page 28*). The waning Moon seems more connected with Hecate, the Hag or Dark Moon, as described in The Moon card (*see page 88*). Using the alchemical model, The High Priestess represents one part of the feminine, or White Queen, which needs to be separated and purified through the alchemical process before she can be merged with the King.

As virgin goddess of the crescent Moon, The High Priestess can be identified with the maiden Persephone – daughter of the Earth Mother Demeter – who was snatched away by the dark god of death, Hades. Having eaten the fruit of the dead, Persephone should never have been able to leave the underworld. However, due to the clever negotiations of Hermes, she was permitted to spend a third of the year with her mother on Earth, during which time nature bloomed and harvests ripened. The remainder of Persephone's time was spent ruling the gloomy kingdom of the dead. This length of time can be equated with the time of gestation necessary before any

Persephone was picking flowers alone when Hades abducted her.

The High Priestess in the Morgan Greer deck shows a veil, which almost hides the fact that there is a pool of water behind her, symbolizing the deep or unconscious mind.

creative process comes to fruition. Ideas and inspirations often swim around in a vague form in the 'back of one's mind' long before they emerge into actuality. It is not unusual to hear someone say, 'I can't talk about my idea yet – it is still too new and unformed.' The obvious creative correlation is with the unborn child, who spends nine months growing and maturing at a great rate but in secret, hidden from the world until the moment of birth, at which time the secret is revealed for all to see.

Feminine Potential

The Lady of the Lake in the Arthurian deck (*below*) sits before a huge pool of water. Legend tells that a female hand rose from the lake, holding the magical sword Excalibur, and it was claimed by Arthur. At the end of his life, Arthur instructed that the sword be returned to the Lady. As Excalibur was thrown back towards the water, The Lady of the Lake's hand appeared out of the lake, caught the sword and turned it three times before plunging both hand and sword back into the depths of the water forever.

The High Priestess card is connected with a longing for knowledge of the otherworld, which Greek myth refers to as Hades and, in psychology, is a symbol of the unconscious mind. The Medieval Scapini deck (*opposite page*) shows The High Priestess seated on a throne between two columns. The column to her left represents the female side, supported by a

The Lady of the Lake card of the Arthurian deck reveals the strength and potency that comes out of feminine passivity – the phallic sword and the womb-like pool of water.

black sphinx and incorporating a mermaid being offered an apple by a serpent, reminding us of the temptation of Eve. This may, in turn, reflect the temptation of Persephone, who left her playmates to look for more beautiful flowers in a lonely place and was abducted by the god of death.

Curiosity and the capacity to be tempted is often associated with the feminine, but, without desire and curiosity, life remains static. The column on her right-hand side is red, for the masculine, and is made up of the fiery symbols of flames and salamanders. Behind her hangs a veil supported by a tiny Sun and Moon – again, a balance of opposites. This is further echoed by the two keys she holds, one gold, the other silver. At her feet, the flowers reflect nature's bounty, while the chequered floor may represent the opposites of day and night, life and death.

II

The Popess

✦ EXERCISE ✦

The High Priestess is the card of calm, inner work, not outer activity. Her energy is contra to 'making decisions' or 'acting constructively'; her world is one of ideas and inspiration.

Keeping this in mind, select a beautiful piece of music that you can use to associate with this card. Breathe deeply and rhythmically. Now allow yourself to visit your own inner world. Using the tarot image as a point to start imaging, let your thoughts wander. Notice how hard it can be to focus on your inside world and how tempting it is to think it 'a waste of time', which could be better spent getting on with a practical task. Keep working with this duality and gradually you will be surprised at what emerges from within you. It will not be easy, and results will not appear immediately. Only in a space of stillness and calm will the Priestess begin to reveal her secrets – they are not freely given and must be earned through consistent effort. Keep a journal to note down all that comes to you.

On the Scapini card, a tiny crescent Moon crowns The High Priestess' headdress. This is the symbol of the Virgin or Maiden, full of potential as yet unfulfilled.

27

THE EMPRESS

THE EMPRESS.

The Empress is an image of potential fulfilled: she is the virgin High Priestess as a mother. Her phase is that of the mature Full Moon and everything about her suggests fertility and creativity. She is depicted in the tarot as Mother Nature, protector of all young defenceless creatures and patroness of all growth. Hers is the richness of nature over which she presides majestically.

Goddess of Nature

The Empress is commonly connected with Demeter, the Greek goddess of nature, the alter-ego of Persephone the maiden. We can see in the many gods and goddesses of Olympus that each personifies one aspect of the whole deity. Persephone is goddess of the dead and, as Demeter, of the living as symbolized by the whole of nature. In the Universal Waite deck (*above*), The Empress is pictured as a mature, confident woman, wearing loose robes suggesting pregnancy, decorated with pomegranates, fruit both of conjugal love and of the dead, reminding us that Persephone and Demeter are different aspects of one multi-faceted goddess. The symbol on the heart-shaped stone is the astrological glyph for Venus, goddess of beauty, love and seduction, yet another face of the archetype of woman, showing her sexual and sensual side. As such, The Empress represents the world of instinctual feelings, natural responses and passions; for emotion rather than thought.

The Waite Empress' twelve-starred crown represents the twelve signs of the zodiac and reflects the different seasons of birth, blossom, fruit and decay, to which each year and all living things are subject. These stages are all under her rulership.

In certain versions of the Dionysus myth, Zeus and his sister Demeter are named as his parents. According to this Orphic version, on hearing of yet another of her husband's infidelities, jealous Hera sent a band of Titans to tear the baby limb from limb. However, Zeus managed to rescue his infant's heart, which he fed to Persephone in the form of pomegranate seeds. This resulted in her impregnation, duly followed by the birth of Dionysus as Iacchus, god of light. The other version of the myth tells of Zeus' affair with Semele, a mortal woman, to whom Hera appeared in the guise of a nurse, urging the maiden to ask her divine lover to appear in his true form. When he did so, his divine radiance burnt her to a crisp, but not before Zeus rescued the foetus and sewed it up in his thigh until it was ready to be born.

The Eleusian mysteries, which honoured the goddesses Demeter and Persephone, took place over two years. The initial May festival celebrated the abduction of Persephone by Hades; the following autumn celebrated Demeter's loss and her mourning. The second May festival celebrated the birth of Dionysus, his short life and violent death; and his joyful rebirth as Iacchus was celebrated in the second autumn festival.

THE EMPRESS

The Sorrowful Mother

The Mythic Tarot (*above*) shows Demeter holding armfuls of corn, identifying her as mother of the harvest, standing in nature's bountiful fields. In addition to being the goddess of all life, health and joy, Demeter has a darker side, that of the sorrowful mother. All mothers are bound to lose their beloved children in some form, as all healthy children grow up and leave home. This is graphically described in the Persephone myth, as the abduction of her daughter is more than Demeter can bear. The great goddess Demeter tore her clothes and wandered across the Earth in a frenzy, searching for her child. Transformed by grief into a white-faced, tear-stained woman, she was no longer recognized by mortals as the glorious Corn Mother.

The Mythic Tarot pictures the Empress standing in a rich corn field crowned with castles and cities. In order to survive we need food, warmth and shelter, all aspects imaged in this card.

Student   *Is The Empress connected with other mother figures?*

Juliet   The suffering of The Empress can also be seen in the agony of Mary, mother of Jesus, whose abject grief could be identified with by all mothers who have suffered the loss of a child. The dual aspect of the joy of creativity and the sorrow of its loss is recognized by all those – male or female – who create some-

The Queen (right) is clearly pregnant, surrounded by the flowers of love and the fruits of the Earth.

The Renaissance deck shows The Empress as Queen of Heaven, holding the orb of power. The peacock in the top right-hand corner links her with Hera.

thing, not just by those women who have a child. Any creative process involves love, commitment and nurture, whether it be to create a baby, a work of art, a literary achievement or song. Once the creation is fully fledged, it leaves; it grows up, gets sold, published, read or sung by someone else, and no longer belongs to the person who gave it life. So the image of the Empress is bitter-sweet, inextricably combining joy and sorrow, life and death, creation and destruction, depending on which face of the goddess the light shines on.

III · L'IMPERATRICE · THE EMPRESS ·

The Watchful Mother

The variety of images used for The Empress reflects the wide-ranging meanings inherent in The Empress card. In the Renaissance deck (*left*), The Empress is depicted as Hera herself, holding the orb of celestial majesty with a peacock above her. When tracking down another of Zeus' infidelities, Hera commanded the monster Argus, who had 100 eyes and only ever closed fifty at one time, to watch Zeus constantly. However, Zeus encouraged Hermes to put Argus to sleep with his magic wand, whereupon the king of the gods slit the monster's throat. Hera put eyes in the tail of a peacock in tribute to Argus and adopted the bird as her attribute. Later, Mary, the Christian queen of Heaven, inherited the peacock as a symbol, the 'eyes' symbolizing the Almighty's ever-watchful gaze.

Queen of Creativity

If we consider the alchemical story (*see page 12*), we see that the barren King mates with the Queen. She is also his sister, indicating that they come from the same root and share the same blood and are thus different sides of the same entity. Hence, in order to become fertile again, the King must become conscious of his feminine side. The result of this merging is the perfect child, and The Empress represents this fertility and new life, heralding a stage of great creativity.

The Wirth deck (*right*) shows the Empress holding a shield engraved with an eagle, symbolizing the soul trapped in the material world. The Empress represents the natural world. Her crown is encircled by a halo of nine stars. This may refer to the nine months of gestation or the nine months of the year that Persephone lived with her mother, when the earth was fruitful.

The Wirth deck shows duality in the wings of spirit and the flower of the Earth. The Full Moon of birth crowns The Empress and the waning Moon of death is at her foot.

• EXERCISE •

The Empress is an earthy card, and it may be helpful to use nature itself to experience her fully. Go outside and note the current season. If it is spring, become intensely aware of the sense of new life and potential emerging from the darkness of winter. Note the activity of animals: birds building nests, lambs playing in the fields, and the budding of plants, bulbs and leaves. Listen to the singing of the birds. If it is summer, observe the strong sensations of smell and colour, the rich abundance of flowers and fruits. If the season is autumn, notice the change in the air, the sudden cold, the damp, earthy smell of rotting leaves and the dwindling warmth of the sun. In winter, be aware of the bleak barrenness of the land, the coldness and darkness of the days. Record your own feelings about the seasons and attach them mentally to the image of The Empress on your tarot deck.

THE EMPEROR

10 arthur

King Arthur is imaged in the Arthurian deck on his throne of authority with his magical sword Excalibur across his knees. Arthur was the champion of Christendom and chivalry, who drew upon all the resources of his land, thus turning his kingdom into one of great strength and vitality.

The Emperor is an image of paternity and male authority. He represents the masculine in the same way that The Empress is a symbol of the feminine. He is usually depicted seated on a throne of some kind, symbolizing material wealth and power, whereas The Empress is depicted blending into nature. The Emperor often carries a sword, which can be regarded as both a phallic symbol and as an indication of leadership.

The Empress and Emperor form a pair of opposites – mother and father, female and male – which combine to bring forth new life. They mirror the earliest creation myths of Sky Father and Earth Mother. In Greek myth, the sky god Ouranos covered the Earth Mother Gaea each night, and each day she produced a child. Unfortunately, Ouranos never liked his earthly children, as none of them could reach the high expectations of the sky god. Likewise, The Emperor symbolizes high-minded ideals; aspiring to excellence.

God of Power

The Emperor is most commonly depicted wearing ceremonial dress and carrying emblems of power, in the form of orbs or globes, signifying his leadership over men and countries. He is an image of authority and strength, and his influence may work for the greater good or evil. As we have seen already, all the tarot cards signify some variation of archetypal power, but power in itself is neutral; it can be used creatively or destructively, depending on the will of its agent.

As an excellent example of male potency, The Emperor is identified with Zeus, the All–Father god. An obvious deity with whom The Emperor can be linked, Zeus was not only father to numerous gods and goddesses, but his divine seed was also sown amongst nymphs and mortals. Despite his initial dislike of humankind, it was not long before their charms began to work on Zeus and his divine nature mingled with that of humans. The Mythic Tarot (*right*) depicts The Emperor as Zeus, wearing the purple robes of majesty and holding in one hand his divine lightning bolts, which he sent to terrify man. In the other hand he carries man's dwelling place, the Earth.

After his struggle with his father, Kronos (*see page 52*), Zeus set up a new democracy on the highest peaks of Mount Olympus, dividing rulership of the oceans, underworld and sky between his brothers Poseidon and Hades, and himself. He made his sister/wife goddess of marriage and childbirth, and gave his other sisters Demeter and Hestia rule over nature, and hearth and home respectively. As a sky god he is linked with the mind and with producing order out of chaos.

THE EMPEROR

Medieval Talismans

In medieval times, it was not uncommon to wear or carry talismans in the belief or hope that they would draw certain energies towards the bearer, depending on the image that appeared on the talisman. For example, it was said that if you wished to attract honour, wealth and success in business transactions, you should carry a talisman bearing the image of a crowned majestic figure.

The *Picatrix*, an ancient Arabic book of magic and sorcery, advocated the use of a talisman featuring the image of a crowned, enthroned king, robed in gold, with a terrestrial globe

The Mythic Tarot shows The Emperor with his sacred bird, the eagle, on his shoulder. The eagle can fly higher than any other bird and has the keenest vision; it is also a symbol of the human soul purified through discipline and will-power.

The use of talismans bearing the image of The Emperor (left) were common in medieval times.

under his feet and a raven perched on his forearm. The instructions for the production of such an image included the suggestion that it should be etched on a ruby at a time and place when the Sun was in the first ten degrees of Leo in the ascendant. Such an image was said to make the bearer '... invincible and honourable, and help to bring their business to a good end, and to drive away vain dreams ...'

◈ **Student** *The Medieval Scapini (below) and Wirth (opposite) decks show The Emperor on a yellow cube. Does this have some special significance?*

◈ **Juliet** The cube itself represents all of the following: the world, the tarot, the Hebrew alphabet and the paths of the Tree of Life. This symbolism, which is explained in detail in Rachel Pollacks' *Seventy-eight Degrees of Wisdom*, arises from the fact that a cube contains twelve edges, six faces, three axes and a centre, all of which adds up to twenty-two, the number of major trumps, Hebrew letters and the paths of the Tree of Life. And because the Tree of Life is said to represent all creation, the cube therefore also symbolizes the entire universe.

The Medieval Scapini deck (*left*) shows The Emperor as ruler of the four elements, which are pictured beneath the platform on which he is seated. The huge natural powers indicated by the elements show winds for Air, volcanoes for Earth, burning buildings for Fire and sinking ships for Water. The platform and its symbol represent the elemental chaos over which The Emperor rules and puts into good order.

The red robes and yellow colours of the cube on the Medieval Scapini card represent power and activity.

IIII

The Emperor

Male and Female Interdependence

As a masculine principle, The Emperor can be connected with Jupiter, the largest planet, said to symbolize expansion, opportunity and growth on the earthly plane. In the alchemical operation, Jupiter's planetary influence comes after Saturn; the mythological son coming to reign once his father has been overthrown. In this respect, Jupiter is like the dawn after the dark night. In our alchemical story, the King has become sterile, but his journey into the underworld and merging with his darker, feminine side produces new life.

There is a constant implication in the tarot images that each one needs the others to be complete. The Emperor, whose thrust is powerful, authoritative and logical, may, without the feelings and intuition of The Empress, become rigid and cold. The Empress, on the other hand, may become overwhelmed by emotions and needs the logic of The Emperor to achieve balance. The Emperor is always battling for perfect achievements, whereas The Empress is more prepared to accept the best that can be hoped for within the limitations of the earthly realm. We need the key aspects of both The Emperor and The Empress in life, for, without high expectations, we would not achieve as much as we would with them; yet we also need to recognize when compromises must be made.

• EXERCISE •

It is important to discover your personal attitude to each image in the tarot. Study the image on your card and note down all the associations you have personally with The Emperor. Is he positive or negative for you? Why do you think this is? Consider the influence of your own father in your life and your attitude to those who have power and authority over you. How do you wield power in your life? Are you a leader or a follower? Consider the ways in which The Emperor may represent both strength and weakness, and see how they apply to yourself. You might even like to construct a talisman using the instructions above. Choose a piece of powerful music to associate with this card. Consider which natural images best represent the essence of The Emperor – for example, mighty oak trees or majestic mountains – and choose one. In this way, you will find the image on the card becomes more alive and potent and personally connected to you.

The Emperor in the Wirth deck is seated on a cube emblazoned with a black eagle, suggesting the combination of spirit and matter.

The bringer of wisdom
Spiritual guidance
Search for meaning
and enlightenment

THE HIEROPHANT

The Hierophant, or High Priest, is known in the old decks as The Pope. Waite renamed the card to pair it with The High Priestess, using the Greek title of Hierophant, meaning 'revealer of holy things'. The High Priest would preside over the Eleusian mysteries of Demeter and Persephone. His presence as a pope or Christian priest in the tarot deck is strange, as the cards were frowned upon by the Church. It is possible that he represents the spiritual aspect of the masculine as The Emperor represents the earthly aspect. The Roman Catholic pontiff took his title from the Latin *pontifex*, meaning the 'bridge builder'. As pope or priest, The Hierophant acts as a mediator between God and man; thus his influence is of a spiritual nature.

Spiritual Mentor

The Hierophant represents the search that propels many of us to find spiritual or religious meaning in our lives in whichever direction we may choose to go. It is that spirit which continues eternally in humankind, although the names of the gods or goddesses may change according to the time and culture. As Alfred Douglas remarks in *The Tarot*, through the inspiration of The Hierophant, 'man's links with God are constantly being renewed and reinterpreted, and thus every age receives its own signposts, freshly painted and pointing out the way'.

The Hierophant is essentially the voice of the masculine spirit and, as we saw with The Emperor, his worldly counterpart, the masculine seeks form and understanding. So The Hierophant becomes the teacher, the guide or mentor who uses the mind to uncover mysteries. Unlike his spiritual partner, the passive High Priestess, who uses stillness and calm, feelings and intuition, to unlock the secrets of the unconscious, The Hierophant seeks, probes, learns, reads and looks to the spoken word for answers. While

V·IL PAPA·THE HIEROPHANT·ᚱ

The Emperor is concerned in an earthly respect with appropriate behaviour and correct responses in the eyes of the world, The Hierophant is concerned with appropriate and correct responses in the eyes of God.

Student *Does The Hierophant stand exclusively for the Christian religion?*

Juliet No, not really. As I said, in Europe at the time the tarot first emerged, Christianity was the dominant faith, although many other beliefs were practised that did not entirely fit within the strict boundaries of the Church. Many aspects of the old pagan gods and goddesses were absorbed into Christianity under different names, and we can see the threads of the pagan deities as they weave their way into the Judeo-Christian motifs.

Let me give you an example. We can see how the Christian Virgin Mary replaced the great goddess of the ancient world. Mary was crowned queen of Heaven and Earth, her festival held in May like those of Demeter and Persphone. She was identified as Mother of the World, and was connected with plants, flowers and fertility like the Greek Earth Mother, Demeter. The rose, which was the sacred flower of first the Egyptian Isis and then the Roman Venus, later came to be one of the Virgin Mary's principal emblems – 'the rose without thorn'. This is a reference to the legend that a thornless rose grew in Eden before Adam and Eve fell from grace. They lost their magic garden and the rose acquired the thorns of sin, yet it retained its beauty and scent to remind man of the lost paradise. The themes are the same but the names have been changed to suit the new religion.

The important issue is that man has always needed a spiritual goal towards which to aspire. And today the Hierophant is interpreted not as a priest belonging to any particular religion but as a representation of the search that propels many of us to find spiritual or religious meaning in our lives. The Hierophant is the card that identifies man's need for a relationship with the spiritual and this is why he is depicted as a Christian priest or pope.

The Visconti deck shows a wise old man wearing the triple-tiered crown of mind, body and spirit. His hand is raised in blessing, two fingers folded down towards the earth, two fingers pointed up towards heaven – as above, so below.

V — THE HIEROPHANT

Achieving Balance

The Hierophant in the Waite deck (*opposite*) wears a golden triple-tiered crown, which symbolizes his wisdom in the realms of the physical, emotional and intellectual, also echoed by his three-pronged staff. At his feet kneel two men, apparently asking his blessing or intercession. One is wearing robes decorated with the red rose of passion, while the other wears the white lily of purity, which reminds us of the balance needed between the masculine and the feminine, the active and the passive. At the feet of The Hierophant lie the crossed keys that can unlock the gates of both Heaven and Hell. This, in turn, reflects the knowledge of good and evil, of conscious and unconscious.

The Morgan Greer deck (*left*) also shows the crossed keys, one gold and one silver, representing the combination of the masculine and the feminine, the Sun and the Moon, which together achieve perfect harmony.

In the Morgan Greer deck, The Hierophant wears a four-layered headdress, which may reflect the four elements which, if combined, form the Quintessence, the perfect fifth. He wears gloves to show that he keeps his hands clean.

Heaven and Earth

The Egyptian king-god Osiris has been connected with The Hierophant, who raises his hand in a traditional sign demanding silence in Egyptian temples. Osiris was a good king who set out to civilize his subjects. He abolished cannibalism and taught his people how to make agricultural tools, cultivate crops and make wine and bread, as well as instructing them in the arts of weaving and music, instituting religious worship and a legal system. His brother, Seth, was jealous of his position and murdered him, but Osiris' wife, Isis, managed to breathe life into

Osiris (right) is depicted with his crook and flail – symbols of his power over death and his nature as a dying-and-rising god.

his corpse long enough for him to impregnate her. When Seth discovered what she had done he cut his brother's corpse into fourteen pieces, which he scattered far and wide. Isis carefully collected the fragments, pieced them together and resurrected him. Although he regained his life and throne, Osiris chose to become lord of the underworld. The dead had to seek permission to enter his kingdom in order to receive continued sustenance of their souls.

Parallels have been drawn between this myth and the Eleusinian, mysteries during which The Hierophant made himself impotent by drinking hemlock – the equivalent to Osiris lying dead. Later a 'sacred marriage' would take place between The Hierophant and The High Priestess – the union of Isis and Osiris. This was followed by a proclamation of the birth of a child – Horus, who took over Osiris' rule on earth. Here is another example of the earthly and spiritual aspects of the masculine, as well as the barrenness, sacred marriage and eventual perfection achieved through the alchemical process.

The Waite Hierophant acts as the middle path between the two figures and the two pillars. The pillars can be seen to represent the opposites of day and night, light and dark.

• EXERCISE •

In order to make contact with the spirit of The Hierophant, start by tracing your own interest and involvement with esoteric subjects such as the tarot. Think about what you were searching for when you picked up your first tarot book – what made you read it? What appealed to you about the subject? What was going on in your life at the time that stimulated your interest? Think about your own attitudes to spiritual and religious matters. Examine your own position on these matters. Make a note of the associations you make with the image on the card and try to select a personal emblem for the card in the form of a piece of music or a colour that can conjure up the essence of The Hierophant for you.

THE LOVERS

VI·GLI AMANTI·THE LOVERS·

The Lovers card usually depicts at least two, often three, people seemingly engaged in some sort of decision. This card has a number of levels of meaning, within the dominant theme of love and desire. In many of the older decks, including the Renaissance (*left*), a familiar figure on the card is Eros, or Cupid, the winged god of desire who became Aphrodite's constant companion. According to Greek mythology, his origins date right back to the beginning of time. Some myths say he was the first-born of all the gods, emerging out of Chaos. The disciples of Orpheus believed him to be the golden-winged son of the wind, hatched from the silver egg of ancient night, born to light the day. Originally he was the awesome god of life-force and desire, although he passed into medieval lore as the mischievous cherub Cupid, whose gold- and lead-tipped arrows could induce passionate love or deep loathing.

The image in the Renaissance deck shows a loving couple standing under an arch. Above the arch are depicted the doves of Venus on the left and Aphrodite and Eros on the right.

The Goddess of Love

The power of beauty and love was originally symbolized jointly by Aphrodite and Eros. From the moment graceful Aphrodite rose out of the sea foam upon a scallop shell near the island of Cyprus, her wondrous beauty evoked desire in all who saw her. Flowers grew up out of every step she took, even in barren sand. Birds longed to imprison themselves in her hair and, at the sight of her, even wild beasts, filled with passion, would leave their hunting to couple with their mates. The most powerful gods and goddesses on Olympus learned to treat her with great deference. They knew that one word from her would be enough to encourage Eros to fire his arrows in their direction, from which none were safe. Aphrodite's loves were many and there were few gods who had not, at one time or another, succumbed to her charms. She wore a magic girdle which, when she unclasped it, made her totally irresistible.

Love and Hate

According to the *Picatrix*, a book of magic spells, a talisman that would bestow beauty and good cheer to its bearer should be constructed while the planet Venus is ascending in the first ten degrees of Taurus, Pisces or Libra. The image should be of a maiden with flowing hair and robes, holding an apple in her right hand (*see Paul Huson's 'The Devil's Picturebook'*). The apple is one of the sacred fruits of Aphrodite/Venus, and a symbol of sexual desire. The prized golden apple brought about both love and death in the Judgement of Paris (*see below*). In the Garden of Eden, a juicy apple enticed Eve and brought about expulsion from Paradise, and in the well-known fairytale of Snow White, a shiny red apple tempted her to disobey the sensible dwarves. The latter story shows the goddess of love in both her guises: as the wicked Queen, jealous of her step-daughter's beauty, and as Snow White, charming, beautiful and easily seduced by the promise of love. Likewise, Aphrodite was gracious to all who worshipped and honoured her, but spiteful and merciless to those who did not. The other side of love is hate and the two are inextricably linked.

THE LOVERS

The Mythic Tarot shows Paris confronted by a difficult choice between three powerful goddesses: Hera on the left, Aphrodite in the middle and Athena on the right. Respectively, they offer him power, love and victory.

The Judgement of Paris

The image on the Mythic Tarot (*above*) refers to the Judgement of Paris, a myth involving Aphrodite and Eros. At the marriage of the sea goddess Thetis and a mortal named Peleus, the goddess of discord had been omitted from the guest list. Angry, she stormed the assembled gods and threw a golden apple into the guests declaring it to be 'for the fairest'. The three goddesses – Hera, Athena and Aphrodite – each offered a bribe to Paris, a mortal shepherd whom Zeus invited to judge the contest. Aphrodite bribed him with love by presenting him with the most beautiful woman in the world, and unclasping her golden girdle. Eros sent a gold-tipped arrow to Paris' heart for good measure. Paris duly awarded the coveted apple to Aphrodite. Unfortunately for Paris, however, the most beautiful woman in the world was Helen of Troy, inconveniently married to King Menelaus,

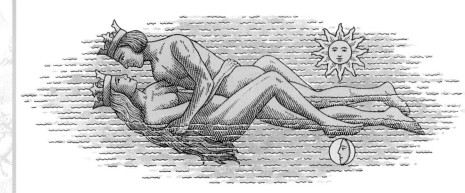

The sacred alchemical marriage between the King and the Queen is represented as harmonious coupling, followed by the King's death and the dark night of the soul.

The Scapini deck shows a winged figure, who appears to be a cross between blind-folded Cupid and Chiron, the wise centaur. His presence may symbolize the difficulty in making prudent decisions when blinded by desire or sexual attraction.

and war broke out when Paris attempted to claim his prize. The slighted goddesses Athena and Hera joined together to take their revenge on Paris by organizing the complete destruction of Troy.

Choosing carefully

The Judgement of Paris myth adds the issue of choice to this card's main theme of love, describing, somewhat graphically, the unfortunate consequences that a hasty decision in love may have.

Student   *So the minute a decision is taken it means something has to change. Is that what this card also means – a change?*

Juliet   It can do. It means that a choice must be taken, which involves giving something up. The root of the word 'decide' means 'slay' (as in 'homicide' or 'suicide'). So, when you choose one thing, you 'kill off' the possibility of another. The choice that faces the young man in The Lovers varies. It may be between mother and lover, childhood and adulthood or, as in the case of Paris, between power, victory and love. Whichever option is picked, the others must be abandoned, and it is often painful. Yet, the positive urge to grow, expand and change can often outweigh the inherent disadvantage and make the move possible.

The issue of choice in The Lovers is central. The Scapini deck (*above*) shows a man and woman holding hands across an abyss. The land on the left is rocky and hard and contains a castle on a mountain top, symbolizing the difficulties to be encountered. On the right is a pleasant terrain with an easily accessible castle. This suggests that love is not just about joy, pleasure and ecstasy but also involves difficult times, pain and heartache. The Wirth deck (*right*) shows Cupid firing an arrow at the young man's heart as he stands between two women. The young man looks down, unwilling to choose, but Cupid's arrow will soon make the decision for him.

Although the images of choice conveyed in The Lovers card may appear simplistic – vice versus virtue, evil versus good – in reality, the choices that need to be considered may be complex. What is important to remember with this card is that all choices have consequences and that those consequences may be far-reaching, which is why serious consideration should be given to seemingly insignificant issues.

One woman on the Wirth card is barefoot and sensual with flowers in her green hair, possibly representing vice. The other is fair-haired and demure, symbolizing virtue.

◆ EXERCISE ◆

Look carefully at the image of The Lovers in your own tarot deck. Use the image to think about the concept of choice, and revisit significant choices you have made in the past. These may be in the field of love or in other areas of life. Think of yourself at the time you made each choice and compare it to your present situation. Did your desires overtake you or did you make your choice in 'the cold light of day'?

Allow yourself to contemplate all the areas associated with this card – ecstasy, beauty, desire, struggle, temptation, longing, loss. Consider how the senses respond to everything over which Aphrodite presides and which encourage attraction: the sight and smell of scented roses, the sound of a harmony, the taste of honey and almonds, and the touch of soft silk or warm water. Combine these sensations for yourself and associate them with this card.

THE CHARIOT

VII·IL CARRO·THE CHARIOT·T

*In the Renaissance deck,
an armoured man sets off
to battle, with the war-
god Ares in one corner
and his sacred bird, the
hawk, in the other.*

The imagery on this card may have been based on the old Roman custom in which a successful general or warrior was processed through the streets in a triumphal car drawn by horses. Such state entries into conquered cities continued in Renaissance Italy, where victors in battle were paraded in glory in richly adorned chariots drawn by powerful horses.

The Fiery Passion of Mars

The Roman god Mars (Greek god Ares) was associated with war and physical mastery. He was hero of the battlefields, accompanied by his henchmen, Phobos (Fright) and Deimos (Panic). Son of Zeus and Hera, Ares was physically strong and handsome, although his character was less attractive. Zeus, in Homer's *Iliad*, says to his son: 'Of all the gods who live on Olympus thou art the most odious to me, for thou enjoyest nothing but strife, war and battles!' Despite this, Ares had enough sex appeal to engage in a long affair with Aphrodite, goddess of love and beauty. Together they produced a child, Harmonia, suggesting that a combination of passion and love could result in harmony.

In the alchemical process, The Chariot is connected with the planet Mars, symbolizing the purifying fire needed to heat the vessel. In astrology, Mars is an active force representing the powerful energy connected with passion, creativity and the sex drive. While the energy of Venus in The Lovers is gentle and beautiful, that of Mars is courageous, positive and vigorous. The need is to balance the two.

Creatures of War

The imagery of a horse-drawn chariot is in itself significant. A symbol of battle, the horse was first produced for the use of humankind by the ocean god Poseidon. When Poseidon and Athena competed over whose name should be taken for a great city, they were each asked to present a gift that would be of great use. The giver of the most appropriate gift would win the contest. Poseidon brought out the first horse ever seen on earth and everyone exclaimed at its power, strength and speed. No one thought Athena could do better, especially when she presented an olive tree. However, she explained that the olive could be used as food, firewood and shelter, but most importantly its leaf was a symbol of peace, while the horse was a symbol of war. The city of Athens was duly named after the goddess who voted for amity not enmity.

In the Wirth deck (*right*), The Chariot was redesigned to depict sphinxes drawing the chariot rather than horses. The sphinx is an enigmatic symbol of duality and contradiction. It is also represented in the Greek myth of Odepius as a deadly creature that seized young men and demanded that they answer a riddle correctly or die. The Chariot suggests that one must solve the riddle of one's own life or be overwhelmed by it.

Taking Control

On the Renaissance deck (*opposite page*) and the Morgan Greer deck (*see page 46*), the two horses drawing the chariot are pulling in opposite directions. One horse is dark, the other light, reflecting the constant presence of opposing impulses that exist in us all. We are all plagued from time to time with passions that oppose reason and it is difficult to balance these strong forces. The Chariot symbolizes the need to gain control of these impulses, although in the Renaissance, Visconti and Wirth decks the charioteer seems to be drawn by the horses, rather than steering them as in the Morgan Greer deck.

If we look at the procession of trumps as a journey through life, the first five trumps are concerned with childhood. The Lovers marks the stage at which The Fool must start to make his own choices and face their consequences. The Chariot symbolizes the point at which he must become master of his own emotions, passions and thought, no matter how contrasting they may be. The charioteer must learn to

The Wirth charioteer is being pulled along by the sphinxes, one dark, one light, representing the never-ending oppositions: creation and destruction, light and dark, passive and active.

VII — THE CHARIOT

be in charge of his life; he must learn to control his horses, rather than let them control him.

> **Student** *Is The Chariot connected with Phaëton who drove the Sun chariot?*

> **Juliet** It is possible that there is a correlation. Phaëton was son of Apollo, the Sun god, whose task it was to carry the Sun around the Earth in a golden chariot. Phaëton was young and ambitious and persuaded his father to let him drive the solar chariot for one day. Apollo was doubtful but agreed in the end, and, somewhat predictably, the youth was quickly overpowered by the strength of the horses, who were naturally delighted to be held so lightly for once. Phaëton lost control of the powerful steeds almost immediately and plunged to his death.

Unlike the other decks shown, the Morgan Greer charioteer has a tight grip on the reins and is controlling the horses.

There are obvious parallels here with adolescence: desire and skill are not equally matched at first and must be carefully managed. In order to truly become an adult one must grow up within as well as physically. At Apollo's shrine at Delphi, the sign over the door said 'know thyself' and 'nothing in excess'.

The Number Seven

The figure on the Visconti Chariot, pulled by winged horses, appears to be female. She holds a globe in one hand and a thin sceptre in the other, indicating power and mastery.

Seven is the number of The Chariot in most decks, and the themes of this number are apparent. Seven is the number of progress, self-expression and independent action. According to Genesis, God made the world in six days and rested on the seventh;

the charioteer celebrates in triumph in his successful creation. The crescent moons on the shoulders of the charioteer on the Morgan Greer deck (*opposite*) also reflect the number seven as each phase of the moon's cycle is complete in seven days and seven is thought to be the number that governs the underlying rhythm of the universe. There are also seven virtues and seven deadly sins. Seven is a prime number, which signifies unity within complexity.

The symbol of a chariot often appears in the lore of talismans. In order to make a talisman that would fill you with strength and provide success in competition or in battle, you should construct an image of an armed and crowned man, carrying a sword and seated in a chariot. This task should be carried out when the planet Mars is ascending in the first ten degrees of its own sign, Scorpio.

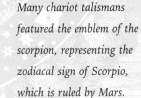

Many chariot talismans featured the emblem of the scorpion, representing the zodiacal sign of Scorpio, which is ruled by Mars.

• EXERCISE •

Try to experience this card as physically as you can. Keep the image of this card in your mind while you carry out your favourite exercise routine. You can use any exercise you like, as long as it represents gaining mastery over weakness. You could choose anything from a punishing round at the gym to a brisk walk in the fresh air. The aim is to put opposing forces in motion and put your own strength and will-power to the test.

Find a piece of stirring music to associate with this card and set an exercise or dance to it. Note your resistances as well and be aware of contradictory impulses. How do you manage them? Do you try to compromise or are you inclined to repress one in favour of the other? As usual, keep a journal of all the observations you make.

JUSTICE צדק

XI — JUSTICE

*The Morgan Greer deck
shows the equal balance
between the sexes – the red
robe is the colour of Mars
and the masculine, while
the green cloak is the
colour of Venus and the
feminine. They are united
by a purple curtain, the
colour of wisdom.*

On each of the tarot representations, the face of
Justice stares out uncompromisingly, as though
seeking the whole truth. Most decks show Justice as a
female figure who holds in balance the masculine
sword and the feminine scales. The Justice card in the
Morgan Greer deck (*left*) emphasizes the idea of balance between male and female by using colour – red for
masculine and green for feminine.

Justice, in the form of logical thought and impartial
decision-making, is a principle that we all need to cultivate. Each of the cards in the Major Arcana represents
a sphere of life that requires development. The Chariot
symbolizes the inner struggle we all experience when
faced with conflicting feelings and emotions within.
Justice symbolizes the capacity we need to enable us to
discriminate, weigh up and judge one set of circumstances against another. The power of the mind can
help us to process the opposing feelings and find a just solution within. The scales are present in so many representations of Justice to
indicate our need to weigh one thing against another in order to
achieve a balance so that two can become one.

The Feather of Truth

The card of Justice has also been associated with the judgement after
death according to Egyptian belief. It was thought that souls of the
dead would be weighed against the feather of Maat, who was the goddess of truth and justice. Her 'feather of truth' was used to weigh the
virtue, or lack of it, found in souls of the dead on the day of their
judgement. The jackal-headed god Anubis was given the task of holding the scales on which the measurement was made. This idea of
weighing the soul filtered into Christianity, and scenes of the Last
Judgement portrayed in the art of medieval times include the souls of
the dead being weighed in scales (*see page 96*).

The Wisdom of Athene

Athene was the wise goddess of the Greeks. She was the daughter of Zeus and Metis, who was Zeus' first wife. Zeus had been warned by an oracle that any child born of his union with Metis would be more powerful than he. So, to prevent such unwelcome competition, Zeus swallowed Metis before she could bear the child she was carrying. Much later, Zeus had a severe headache and begged Hephaistos, the god of the forge, to split open his skull. Athene, fully grown and clothed in battle dress, sprang out of her father's head. She took her place among the other Olympians as a warrior goddess but, unlike Ares, whom we met in the Chariot (*see page 44*), she preferred strategy to bloodshed on the battlefields. Although she recognized the necessity of fighting to uphold matters of principle and to preserve the truth, she despised Ares' battle tactics of brute force, preferring diplomacy and logic. As a result she was worshipped as the goddess of dispassionate justice.

Born from the head of her father, Athene was a symbol of rational thought and the capacity for impartial judgement. This faculty separated humankind from the animal kingdom and was therefore seen by the Greeks as a divine attribute. As Athene was not born from a woman in the usual way, she was not associated with the instinctual nature of the feminine. She maintained her chastity and was unconcerned with passion, either physical or emotional. Her power resided in the mind and she used her intelligence to civilize humankind. As we saw in the Chariot, her gift to man was peace in the form of the olive tree. She taught men the art of taming horses – the animals of war – as well as encouraging skills, such as weaving and embroidery, thus combining useful work with artistic creation.

The Romans worshipped Athene under the name of Minerva, which is derived from the root 'mens' or 'manas', meaning the mind. Minerva's sacred bird was the owl, traditionally connected with wisdom, and also a symbol of clear perspective because the owl can see in the dark and has wide-ranging vision.

Athene sprang into being fully formed and armed from her father's head, establishing her as a goddess of the mind.

JUSTICE

The Mythic Tarot shows Justice as the goddess Athene. The black and white checks on the floor symbolize the mind's ability to sort dark and light into orderly patterns.

The Number of Balance

Justice was traditionally given the number eight in the tarot, although Waite changed the order of Strength and Justice, giving Strength eight and Justice eleven. Eight was known to the Greeks as the number of justice because it is made up of equal divisions of even numbers, which suggests balance. Justice was also one of the four cardinal virtues in life.

> **Student** *What are the four virtues? I thought there were supposed to be seven?*

> **Juliet** Early Christian theologians suggested that the virtues of Justice, Strength, Prudence and Temperance occurred naturally in humanity without God's intervention. The other virtues, Faith, Hope and Charity, were thought to come directly from God. These join the first four to make up the seven virtues. However, the notion of four virtues seems to date back beyond Christianity to the Greek philosophers, Aristotle and Plato. The virtues later passed from Greece to Rome and became an integral part of Latin memory-training systems (*see page 9*).

The Four Elements

Aristotle explained the formation of the physical world through the four elements – namely Fire, Air, Water and Earth. He maintained that each element was composed of two properties. He held that the properties of Fire were dryness and heat; Air's properties were heat and fluidity; Water's properties were fluidity and coldness; and Earth's properties were coldness and dryness. Aristotle went on to argue that the elements could blend into each other by means of their shared properties. For example, Fire blends into Air by heat; Air into Water by fluidity, and so on. In this way each element could be transformed into another by combining with an opposite element and using two of its qualities. Thus Earth, the properties of which are cold and dry, could be formed by combining the coldness of Water with the dryness of Fire. The four elements (and the four cardinal virtues) are reflected in the cards of the tarot in the following way. In the Major Arcana Justice is linked with Air; The Hermit with Earth; Strength with Fire; and Temperance with Water. In the Minor Arcana the suit of Swords is linked with Air, Pentacles with Earth, Wands with Fire, and Cups with Water.

In the alchemical process, Air represents the qualities that are both gaseous and subtle. The gases in the vessel are symbolized by rising and falling birds; as liquids boil, gases escape and coalesce like crystallized birds on the walls of the vessel (*see M.E. Warlick's 'The Philosopher's Stones'*). As we have seen, Air is the element connected with the mind, which must be used to moderate physical activity in the same way that Air must be added with care in order to moderate Fire and its effects on the alchemical process.

The Medieval Scapini deck shows a woman seated between two pillars, representing the need for balance between opposites. Two suns symbolize illumination and clarity of vision. The side panels show scenes of the four seasons, during each of which balance must be achieved.

• EXERCISE •

As Justice is the card of Air, it would be a good idea to start working with this image using breathing exercises. Lie flat on the floor with your hands resting near the base of your ribs, where your diaphragm is. Breathe normally for a few minutes. Now fill your lungs more deeply and observe the difference between deep and shallow breath. As we inhale, we take in oxygen-rich air and, as we exhale, we rid ourselves of impure, stale air. Justice is connected with Libra, the astrological sign that rules the kidneys, the organ that purifies the body. Use this breathing exercise to purify the mind. Now concentrate on thinking. Take a current problem and apply logical thought to it. Draw a pair of scales and place the advantages of the situation on one side and the disadvantages on the other. See how the scales balance as your seek your solution. Become aware of the refreshing quality of Air physically and mentally as you allow yourself to process ideas actively.

THE HERMIT

VIIII

l'Ermite

*The Wirth deck shows
a serpent at the feet of
an old man. Serpents
symbolize wisdom, old
age and renewal, as they
regularly shed their skins.
At this point they are very
vulnerable until the new
skin has hardened.*

The Hermit heralds a time for reflection and introspection in the quest for deeper understanding.
His solitude can be a strength and his patience brings
peace and acceptance. He has been connected with the
virtue of Prudence and the element of Earth.

The Fool, Matured

The image of The Hermit is generally that of an old
man with a long beard, cloaked and hooded, carrying
a lantern. It calls to mind the archetype of the wise old
man. He is, in fact, The Fool approaching mid-life. The
serpent in the Wirth deck (*left*), waiting for its new
skin to harden, can be seen as a symbol of middle age.
The Hermit stands between youth (the discarded
skin) and old age (the renewed skin).

In the first flush of youth, The Fool steps off the
edge of a precipice in broad daylight with his face
upturned and his staff held lightly. As the older and
wiser Hermit, he has learned many salutary lessons and now he looks
carefully where he is going and uses his staff for support. He often
carries a lamp, symbolically illuminating the darkness. His heavy cloak
and hood shield him against the cold, as he makes his solitary journey.

Associations with Kronos

The Hermit is most commonly associated with the Greek myth of
Kronos (Saturn to the Romans). Kronos was the son of the Sky Father,
Ouranos, and Earth Mother, Gaea. Sadly, the sky god Ouranos did not
find his Earthly children appealing, so he imprisoned them in Earth's
body. Eventually Gaea found this situation intolerable and gave her
son Kronos a silver sickle with which to castrate his father. Kronos
obliged, overthrowing Ouranos and liberating his incarcerated siblings. However, Kronos did not learn from his father's mistakes. He

ruled a Golden Age and wished his great reign to continue forever. Hearing that his children would one day overthrow him, Kronos tried to cheat fate by swallowing his children at birth. However, history has a habit of repeating itself, and his wife, like his mother, refused to allow all her progeny to be eaten. She hid her last born, Zeus, and when he reached manhood Zeus overthrew Kronos and freed his brothers and sisters. Kronos was then banished to the Isles of the Blessed where he ruled as the god of time and old age. In fact, they say he is ruling there still, patiently waiting for his Golden Age to return.

The scythe of Kronos (left) is shaped like a crescent Moon, symbolizing the cycles of time.

The Waite deck shows the Hermit on the top of a mountain, indicating a wide range of vision. He is old and bowed down with knowledge and experience, yet his lantern gleams with the star of hope.

Student *I thought hermits mostly lived in monasteries or hermitages. Why is he so often pictured in an open landscape?*

Juliet It is true that most decks show a figure on a journey, although, in fact, most real hermits find a place of stability in a hermitage or hut. That he is usually depicted on a journey indicates that the tarot Hermit is still searching for that place of repose, so this card may reveal that part of the journey is as yet unclear.

The associations of this card are solitude and introspection, which often take place on an inner level rather than on an outer. Not many of us actually become hermits in the true sense of the word by

THE HERMIT.

IX THE GRAIL HERMIT

The Arthurian deck, exceptionally, shows The Hermit sitting in repose before his hut. He has found peace in solitude.

retreating from society; yet this card marks the phase in which, often in the second half of life, we turn towards the inner world in a search for meaning and enlightenment of a different kind. The Arthurian deck (*left*) makes an exception to the general rule, showing a hermit in residence, the wise man who has found a comfortable existence in solitude. The Grail Hermits fulfilled important tasks for those on the quest for the Holy Grail: they admonished the lazy, explained the wonders and provided welcome shelter on the journey

However, above all, The Hermit seeks understanding of the meaning of life. Alfred Douglas, in *The Tarot*, quotes the philosopher Schopenhauer in relation to The Hermit: 'Life may be compared to a piece of embroidery, of which, during the first half of his time, a man gets sight of the right side, and during the second half, of the wrong. The wrong side is not so pretty as the right, but it is more instructive; it shows the way in which the threads have been worked together.'

The Search for Inner Understanding

In alchemy, the base material is often lead, a substance ruled by the planet Saturn. The objective of the alchemical work was to transmute something ordinary, such as lead, into something extraordinary, such as gold. The task of the alchemist involved painstaking attention to every stage and detail: the positions of the planets, the balance of ingredients and the temperatures. Above all, it involved patience to allow each stage to unfold as it should. The Renaissance deck (*opposite page*) shows Hephaistos, the ugly, yet gifted, god of the forge and metal-work. His creations were exquisite and, despite his lameness and lack of social graces, his work enchanted the Olympians, who insisted he remain on Olympus – normally they refused to allow anyone who was not beautiful to live with them.

The quest for personal transformation and enlightenment was always a part of the alchemical philosophy. As M.E. Warlick says in her book *The Philosopher's Stones*: 'Hidden among the puzzling descriptions in old manuscripts is the continuing thread of alchemy's high spiritual purpose. The creation of gold is secondary to the quest for self-knowledge and self-perfection that begins as the alchemist engages in the work. The more one grapples with the alchemical process, with its inevitable triumphs and disappointments, the more one comes to understanding the Self. Primal Matter, the Philosopher's Stone and the alchemist are one.'

In today's fast-moving world, it is difficult to find the time to engage with the process of inner understanding. Increasingly, our culture urges us to find 'instant' solutions, and technological advances encourage us to believe that we can. However, although our external world is changing rapidly, our inner worlds are not. We still need the slow, quiet introspection of The Hermit as much now as we did in the Middle Ages.

IX · L'ERMITA · THE HERMIT ·

In the Renaissance deck The Hermit carries an hourglass, which reflects his connection with Father Time who swallows his children.

• EXERCISE •

The exercises for The Hermit involve connecting with discipline and patience. The herb sage was connected with longevity and with the planet Saturn. It may help you to smell sage, either fresh or as an essential oil, to focus on this card. Soft, slow music might also be helpful: try listening to some medieval chants or hymns to help you meditate on the image of The Hermit.

Having prepared yourself, find a quiet spot, sit down and take time to relax. Breathe deeply and rhythmically, concentrating on each in and out breath. Now take the image of The Hermit and contemplate it with deep seriousness. Allow your own personal associations to emerge in the forefront of your mind. Note how you feel about the image. Is it comforting or frightening? How do you feel about the issues The Hermit symbolizes – solitude, patience, meditation? Think about your own attitudes and make notes.

THE WHEEL OF FORTUNE

The oldest image found on the Visconti deck is of the blind goddess Fortuna, turning the wheel so that men's fortunes rise and fall at random.

The Wheel of Fortune is an image of the one constant in life, which paradoxically is change. Like The Hermit, this card has also been connected with the virtue of Prudence.

According to Greek mythology, the fate or destiny of every human was governed by the three spinners known as the Moirae or Fates, who spun, measured and cut the length of each man's life. The word *moira* means 'portion', so once again we see a connection with the lunar cycle and its three phases: youth, maturity and old age. Like the Moon, the wheel is round and ever changing.

Fortune's Rise and Fall

The Romans believed that man's life was not his own but governed totally by the whim of the goddess Fortuna. She is shown on the Renaissance deck (*see page 58*), standing before a wheel made up of the Major Arcana, symbolizing the various stages of life. The Visconti deck (*left*) illustrates the same point clearly by means of the four figures attached to a wheel. The figure on the left rises, looking hopeful, and the gold lettering near him reads *Regnabo*, meaning 'I will reign'. The figure at the top sits triumphantly with a sign *Regno*, meaning 'I reign'. On the right, the figure falls, and the lettering reads *Regnavi* or 'I have reigned'; while a fourth wretched figure lies beneath the wheel with a sign saying *Sum sine regno*, which means 'I am without reign'.

The figures rising and crowning have asses' ears, which may refer to the myth of King Midas, the foolish king who first wished for the golden touch, and narrowly escaped with his life, before awarding Pan a prize in a musical competition between the goat god and Apollo, the Sun god. Apollo, in turn, awarded him asses' ears for his stupidity. The theme here is one of 'pride comes before a fall'.

Ever-revolving Wheel

WHEEL of FORTUNE.

The image of the wheel may also come from the fiery wheel onto which Zeus bound Xion. Xion was a man much favoured by Zeus, who was invited to live with the gods on Olympus. However, after a while Zeus began to suspect Xion of loving Hera, his wife. Zeus made an image of Hera out of clouds and the unfortunate Xion made love to the cloud maiden, who bore him a son that was half-horse and half-man – the first centaur. Zeus punished Xion severely by binding him to a burning wheel on which he was destined to spin forever.

A Celtic myth that relates to the wheel is the vision of King Arthur, who, the night before his final battle had a dream of a splendid king seated in triumph at the top of a wheel. Abruptly, the goddess of fortune turned the wheel, which crushed the king under its might. Arthur realized that no matter how much wealth, power or status a man might have, his life is always subject to greater forces – the power of God.

 Student   *The imagery on the Universal Waite deck (above) is very different to the others – there are no human figures at all.*

Juliet   That's right. Waite used a mixture of Egyptian and biblical figures to illustrate his wheel, emphasizing a theme of death and rebirth. The snake on the left is Seth, the Egyptian god who brought death into the world and killed the good king Osiris (*see page 38*). On the right, the jackal-headed figure is Anubis, guide to the dead souls and thus a bringer of new life. On the top, a sphinx represents Horus, son of Osiris and god of resurrection. This wheel shows the transition of death through to rebirth, loss through to gain.

The four creatures in each corner appear to have been drawn from the biblical vision of Ezekiel (Ezekiel 1:10). They also reflect the four fixed elements in astrology: Taurus, Leo, Scorpio and Aquarius, representing Earth, Fire, Water and Air, respectively. The zodiac is another image of a great, ever-revolving wheel, which marks a passage

The Roman letters on the Waite card can read TARO or ROTA (Latin for 'wheel'), while the other lettering spells out the great name of God as it appears in the Torah *– Y, H, V, H (yod he vau he). Without vowels the name is unpronounceable, thus God's 'true' name remains a secret.*

X·LA FORTVNA·CHANCE

through time by season. The elements symbolize those used in alchemy and the symbols on the spokes of the wheel are also alchemical: from the top in a clockwise direction they read: mercury, sulphur, water and salt. The combinations of the four different elements produces a perfect fifth.

Inner Driving Force

As the hub remains still, the turning rim of the wheel represents time marching on, year after year, with the Sun, Moon and planets revolving in the zodiacal wheel, ever-changing and yet always the same. Seasons follow each other and yet, even though each phase of the wheel recurs, the wheel constantly moves forward. Life is made up of opposite factors: day and night, expansion and contraction, blossom and decay.

The true self may be likened to the hub, unchanging and often unnoticed, and yet the central force that enables our lives, or the rim, to move forwards. So it is our deep, or unconscious, self which often invites a change of circumstance into our lives. Although we do not always like that change, we can usually (most often with hindsight) see the opportunity for growth involved. It follows that the more we get to know our inner selves, the more opportunity for choosing the direction of our lives we will have.

On the Renaissance card, Fortune points to the right-hand figure who is on the side of the castle and facing upwards, while the left-hand figure is destined for the abyss as gestured by the goddess.

This is similar to the Indian doctrine of karma, which teaches that there is no such thing as chance and that everything has a cause and an effect. The law of karma teaches that our

The zodiac represents the Great Wheel of the Visible Universe. We can see the Sun's progress through each sign.

good fortune, or otherwise, is a direct result of our actions and choices, either in this life or previous lives, and that we must continue to ride the wheel of life until the soul reaches the highest level of spiritual evolution, at which point we may be liberated.

X — WHEEL OF FORTUNE

The three figures on the Morgan Greer card (*right*) have been connected with the virtue of Prudence, which, according to the Roman writer Cicero, had three parts: memory, intelligence and foresight. Together they provide an understanding of the past, present and future. Cicero's definition of Prudence is knowledge of the good, the bad and the neither good nor bad.

The Wheel of Fortune in a reading denotes a change in circumstances, which we may or may not wish for. What is important, however, is how we respond to that change – whether we are able to move with the current positively or whether we seek to blame fate for upsetting the proverbial apple cart. Whatever we do, the wheel turns from triumph to disaster and back in a never-ending flow.

The Morgan Greer deck shows three figures – two rejoicing in their position at the top of the wheel while a third falls into an abyss.

✦ EXERCISE ✦

Consider your own life and reflect on a completed whole. Think about the different phases of initiation, fulfilment and completion that have taken place during your life. Track back the feelings from the beginning to the present and notice all the changes.

You can choose the course of a relationship, a piece of work or a period of study as examples of following the wheel as it makes its progress, passing the four figures as it makes its rotation. You might also like to think of the various phases of fortune as the seasons of spring, summer, autumn and winter, symbolizing by turn new growth, fruition, decay and death. Consider your own part in the process: what do you feel you chose and what do you feel was 'fate'. As always, keep careful notes of your findings.

STRENGTH

XI • LA FORZA • STRENGTH •

The figure of Heracles breaking the lion's jaw in the Renaissance deck was rendered in the style of Michaelangelo.

The image of a human struggling with the king of the beasts is one that suggests man's struggle to tame his own animal instincts. Strength is the third of the cardinal virtues and, as such, hints at inner as well as physical strength. The contest between man and lion echoes the struggle of man with the opposing horses as represented in The Chariot – the conflict between instinctual desires and the conscious mind.

Strength, or fortitude, is another of the four cardinal virtues. The virtues were often portrayed in medieval and Renaissance art as female, in many cases dressed for battle against vice. The tarot often portrays Strength as feminine as in the illustrations of the Wirth deck (*opposite*) and the Waite deck (*see page 63*).

The Labours of Heracles

The image that appears on many of the older decks, including the Renaissance deck (*above*), refers to Heracles' (also known as Hercules) fight with the Nemean lion. Heracles was the son of Zeus and a mortal woman, Alcmene. Zeus' jealous wife Hera hated Heracles passionately, wishing him dead – she was forever tracking down Zeus' illegitimate offspring so she could eliminate them. From the moment he was born, however, it was clear that he was the son of a god, so great was his strength and physical prowess. When Heracles was only eight months old, Hera sent two huge snakes to choke him in his cradle, but the sturdy infant strangled both serpents with casual ease. Enraged, Hera continued to torment Heracles, at one point driving him mad with a rage so great that he murdered his wife and sons. After the dreadful murders, his madness left him and Heracles was faced with the appalling consequences of his fury.

In order to make amends for this hideous crime, Heracles undertook twelve labours, the first of which was to kill the Nemean lion using only his bare hands. All the labours were extremely arduous

The woman on the Wirth card calmly deals with a very fierce-looking lion. Her floppy rimmed hat repeats the figure of eight or lemniscate, *which means eternity.*

and most were life-threatening. Unlike Ares, god of war (*see page 44*), who enjoyed the heat of the battlefield and liked conflict for its own sake, Heracles' had to meet and master his challenges as an individual and each struggle brought him a personal victory. Once he had strangled the Nemean lion, he skinned the beast and used its impenetrable pelt as a cloak, which rendered him invincible. In this way he made personal use of his victory.

Heracles can be seen as a solar hero as his labours equalled the time the Sun takes to pass through each zodiacal sign. He was obliged to struggle with many difficult opponents and situations as he worked through his labours, in the same way as The Fool must pass through each stage of the Major Arcana. Each of the cards reflect a 'labour' and represent a lesson The Fool must learn. In Strength, The Fool must begin to face his darker side.

Student *It sounds as if Strength is like The Chariot, only more so!*

Juliet You could say that. As we move through the cards, each of the Major Arcana reflects the next deeper stage as the mystery of life intensifies. In the first half of life, we tend to spend

61

*In the Mythic Tarot,
Heracles is pictured
strangling the lion with
his bare hands, as the
lion's pelt was too thick for
sword or club to penetrate.
The cave represents the
first encounter with the
unconscious mind.*

time discovering, learning about and enjoying the external side of life. We happily take this at face value with little need for introspection, and this phase of life is reflected in the first seven cards.

If we think of The Fool on his journey through the Major Arcana, it is possible to envisage his childhood with The Magician as teacher, The Empress and Emperor as earthly parents, and the High Priestess and Hierophant as heavenly forces. His struggles in love with The Lovers and conflict with The Chariot are clear. However, when he reaches Justice, he needs to do more than act and react. He must think about things impartially. The Hermit urges a search for meaning in the inner world. His attitude changes further with The Wheel of Fortune, as he realizes that he can both rise and fall. Now, Strength is vital in order to provide him with the self-discipline and courage he will need to face the next stage, which is the underworld journey.

STRENGTH

Managing Instinctual Needs

The image on the Strength card usually depicts a figure, male or female, in hand-to-hand combat with a large lion. The lion is a symbol of natural power, might and passion; so the man or woman seeking to tame or subjugate it must struggle forcefully. The lion is also an image of what Jung called the shadow, that is, the darker side of our personality, the side that we least like. If this unconscious energy can be brought into consciousness and understood, it can be liberating. The lion represents instinctual wishes and passions that can fuel the personality with vigour if they are not repressed or denied. However, the passions and desires that add fire to the personality also need to be controlled, so self-discipline must be acquired.

Many tarot decks show the figure simply holding the lion's jaws open, rendering the beast harmless. The instinctual needs and desires are not wrong in themselves, but they do need to be managed otherwise they can become destructive. The way to do this is first to recognize the need or desire and then find ways of fulfilling it in the most constructive way possible.

Balancing Masculine and Feminine

The Waite deck (*right*) shows the alchemical symbolism in its image of the girl closing the lion's jaws. The lion represents the masculine, fiery, active principle of Philosophic Sulphur or the Red King, while the graceful maiden represents the feminine, watery, passive principle of Philosophic Mercury or the White Queen. Out of the sexual union between the King and Queen, the lower elements of sulphur and mercury can transform into the higher elements of gold and silver.

The lovely maiden depicted on the card may be a representation of Cyrene, who served the Moon goddess Artemis, and was spotted by the Sun god Apollo as she struggled courageously with a lion. He fell in love with her immediately and whisked her off in his chariot to North Africa.

The maiden on the Waite card closing the lion's mouth wears white robes of purity with red roses, reflecting the theme of the feminine and masculine principles in balance. The horizontal figure of eight is reminiscent of The Magician card.

• EXERCISE •

Take out your card of Strength and feel your way into the image. Try to imagine the struggle and think of any kind of situation where you tend to struggle with yourself. You may like to concentrate on a particular personal struggle.

Consider the process that goes on within you if one part of you desires something that is not altogether good for your body, for example, an alcoholic drink, a chocolate bar or a cigarette, while another side of you thinks you would be better off without the substance. How do you resolve such an inner conflict? Which side of you generally wins such battles?

Now think about the way you respond personally to discipline. Are you able to discipline yourself or do you need others to do it for you? Can you usually find a satisfactory compromise? Make notes about your feelings and observations that arise from this exercise.

THE HANGED MAN

XII · L'IMPICCATO · THE HANGED MAN

The curious figure of The Hanged Man, who appears on most decks, is of a man hanging by one foot from a gibbet, commonly made of two tree trunks and a crossbar. Despite the unusual position, his face is peaceful and composed, so the image is a calm one. The card infers that at this stage of his journey The Fool must adopt this peculiar upside-down position in order to look at life from a new perspective and there-by reach a new level of spiritual and psychological understanding. Through the Strength card (*see pages 60–63*), the Fool has struggled with the lion within – his shadow – and realized that he is more than just his conscious self – the part of himself with which he has wholly identified so far. He is now aware that he also possesses an unconscious side, which he is only just beginning to discover. This card marks the beginning of his exploration of that unconscious.

In the Renaissance card, a man is suspended by one leg beneath a small figure at top right, representing the Titan Prometheus.

Voluntary Sacrifice

There are numerous myths from which this card could have derived its symbolism. The notion of sacrificing something in order to gain something more valuable is reflected in the story of the Greek Titan Prometheus, who suffered intense torture after having stolen fire for his beloved creation, mankind. He defied the orders of Zeus, who for-bade anyone other than the gods to benefit from divine fire. Zeus pun-ished him by stretching him out on a mountain top where an eagle ate his liver. Every night the liver would grow again, enabling the eagle to repeat the torture every day. Jesus sacrificed himself on the cross in order to give mankind eternal life. While Norse myth tells of Odin, who hung himself upside down on the World Ash tree for nine nights in order to gain wisdom and insight. In each of these examples, the key is voluntary sacrifice: a choice is made to relinquish something of value in order to gain something far more valuable.

The Hanged Man has also been connected with Dionysus (*see page 19*), who was dismembered before he could be reborn as Iacchus. In Greece, small effigies of Dionysus were often hung in trees in the hope that this 'death' would ensure the fertility of the land. In Sumerian rites, an effigy representing the god Attis would be hung in a pine tree. The tree was regarded as a symbol of the mother, the source of all life. Consequently all those who died on a tree were thought to be reunited with their source.

xii the wounded king

Thinking of Others

The Arthurian deck (*right*) moves away from traditional imagery in its depiction of a wounded king, representing the redemptive sacrifice of the Grail mysteries. The King is seriously hurt, yet his suffering opens him to wisdom and insight. According to Arthurian legend, Parsifal, Seeker of the Holy Grail and one aspect of The Fool (*see page 18*), arrives at a castle in the middle of a wasted barren land. There he meets the wounded king and is required to ask a question. Up until this stage, Parsifal – still The Fool – has always been told what to think and how to act by others. Consequently, when asked to think for himself he finds he is unable to do it. As he does not know what question to ask, he remains silent and in doing so fails the test. The questions that he should have asked the king are: 'Lord, what ails thee?' and 'Lord, whom does the Grail serve?'

The Hanged Man symbolizes the point in the journey of The Fool when he can no longer rely on others for their wisdom or opinions; instead, his own reflection is required. Parsifal must become aware of the king's wounds and the wasteland that surrounds him before the healing can take place. In other words, he must learn compassion and to think not only of himself. Parsifal fears that if he admits that he does not know what question to ask, he will look stupid, thus revealing that he is more interested in his own ego image than the tragedy that faces him. Likewise, the tarot Fool must first know his own weakness and wounds in order that he may take the right steps towards healing them. The ego must die in order to reborn.

The Arthurian deck shows a forest clearing. Here, surrounded by banners, the king lies bleeding, his faithful hound at his side.

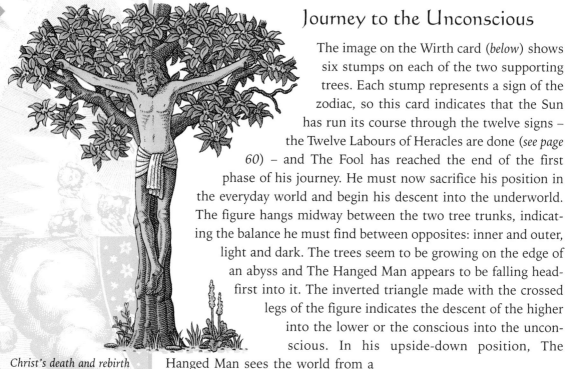

Christ's death and rebirth coincides roughly with the Spring Equinox, the beginning of a new astrological year.

On the Wirth card, coins fall from The Hanged Man's pockets. He has abandoned all expectation of worldly riches and is prepared to sacrifice them for spiritual wealth, just as the ferryman must be paid in order to enter the kingdom of the dead.

Journey to the Unconscious

The image on the Wirth card (*below*) shows six stumps on each of the two supporting trees. Each stump represents a sign of the zodiac, so this card indicates that the Sun has run its course through the twelve signs – the Twelve Labours of Heracles are done (*see page 60*) – and The Fool has reached the end of the first phase of his journey. He must now sacrifice his position in the everyday world and begin his descent into the underworld. The figure hangs midway between the two tree trunks, indicating the balance he must find between opposites: inner and outer, light and dark. The trees seem to be growing on the edge of an abyss and The Hanged Man appears to be falling headfirst into it. The inverted triangle made with the crossed legs of the figure indicates the descent of the higher into the lower or the conscious into the unconscious. In his upside-down position, The Hanged Man sees the world from a wholly different perspective.

Belief in Sacrifice

In the alchemical story (*see page 12*), at this stage the King, who was born perfect, has become sterile and the lands he rules are barren. Richard Cavendish observes in *The Tarot* that alchemy has had an important influence on interpretations of The Hanged Man. Levi referred to him as 'the great and unique *athanor*, which all can use, which is ready to each man's hand, which all possess without knowing it'. The *athanor* was the alchemist's furnace and was thought to be the fierce heat of the

alchemist's own transforming fervour. In other words, we are the *athanor*, and our bodies are the vessels within which the alchemical process can take place. The Hanged Man symbolizes the approach of the 'blackening' or *nigredo*, and marks the end of the first stage. The alchemist approached the alchemical process with a high purpose in mind; he wished to find the valuable treasure, or elixir. He believed that the many difficulties, disappointments and sacrifices that he would undoubtedly encounter during the course of the work would ultimately be worthwhile.

When The Hanged Man appears in a reading, it denotes a time of personal choice in which something of great personal value must be relinquished in order to gain something of even greater value. The sacrifice involves an act of faith as there is no guarantee of the outcome. It is not like shopping when you are told the cost of an item and make a clean exchange. The sacrifice must be made without a promise of gain, only a belief that it will be worthwhile.

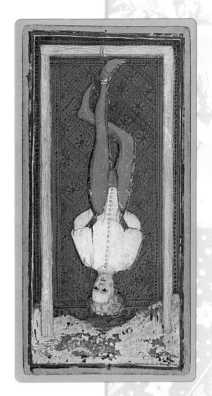

• EXERCISE •

Study the image of The Hanged Man in your chosen deck closely and allow your mind to wander freely over all the associations. Think about all the issues of sacrifice that have occurred during your life. How many instances can you can recall in which you made a conscious sacrifice in regard to a relationship, financially, career-wise or for your family? Consider the difference in the feelings aroused within yourself when you choose to give something up to those triggered when someone else forces you to give something up.

See how many different ways you can look at your life. The Hanged Man card is about seeing your life or important issues from another perspective. How difficult or easy is it for you to view your situation from another point of view?

Like most images of The Hanged Man, the Visconti figure hangs by one foot, the part of the body assigned to Pisces, the last sign of the zodiac. The Sun passes through Pisces during the Christian period of Lent, the preparation for Christ's crucifixion.

DEATH מות

DEATH

The Mythic Tarot shows three figures before Hades. The man and woman offer bribes of wealth. The child offers a narcissus, associated with death because of its ghostly colour and its emergence each spring after the death of winter.

The image of Death as a skeleton is the most common one in the tarot, although the Waite deck (*opposite page*) shows the skeleton in armour, and the Mythic Tarot shows Hades as the god of the underworld welcoming in the new souls. In many cases, Death is cutting down or trampling over the bodies of men, women and children, young and old alike, symbolizing that he comes to us all in due course.

The skeleton of Death is often pictured with a reaping scythe, a reference to Saturn, god of time (*see page 52*). In the Death card, 'time' becomes 'mortality', which can be linked with the Moirae, or the three spinners of fate, encountered with the Wheel of Fortune card (*see page 56*). The masculine version of the Moirae was the ancient god of the night, Moros, who also had a triple personality and was often accompanied by his brothers Thanatos (Death) and Hypnos (Sleep).

According to the Greeks, after Zeus overthrew his father, Kronos, he divided rulership of the sky, ocean and underworld between himself and his two brothers. He took the sky, Poseidon took the ocean, and Hades became Lord of the Dead. Although he was not as colourful as his brothers, Hades possessed the greater power because his law was irrevocable. Once a soul entered his kingdom, no god, not even Zeus himself, could retrieve it.

River of Transformation

Richard Cavendish in *The Tarot* connects Death with the Hindu god Shiva, the Destroyer, but not as the one who ends life, but rather as the one who has the power to annihilate the form of something without destroying its essence. Shiva is also connected with sexuality and regeneration as well as destruction – the Elizabethans referred to the collapse of the phallus after orgasm as the 'little death'. His rule is of a world whose rhythm changes life into death and death into life.

Shiva is the god who fertilized the sacred river Ganges and, in a number of decks, a river is featured in Death. It was believed that the souls of the dead were ferried across a stream or river to reach their new place of rest. In Egyptian myth, the boat was manned by the jackal-headed Anubis, god of embalming, while the Greek dead were in the charge of Charon, who insisted on an obulus – a Greek coin – in payment for his services. In Christian hymns, the river Jordan is referred to as the crossing point to the Promised Land. The river itself is a symbol of transformation: water is drawn up from the sea to form clouds, falls to Earth as rain and returns to the sea in rivers.

The Even Hand of Death

The representations of Death in the tarot are stark. The skeleton is an image of the toughest and most resistant part of the body: the flesh decays but the bone remains. The Waite deck (*below*) shows Death on a white horse riding roughshod over a king, ignoring the entreaties of a bishop, while a maiden turns her head at the inevitable. This shows that death comes to us all, no matter how famous, rich, beautiful, young or powerful we are; such worldly currency does not impress him. Death is dressed in black and rides a white horse.

On the Waite card, a boat can be glimpsed on the river, which may be the Styx, whose waters flowed with new life as well as death.

Black is the colour of death as black absorbs all colour and death absorbs all life. White repels all colours and is a sign of spiritual purity. He carries a black flag with an emblem of the Mystic Rose, which has five petals, representing the four elements plus the spirit of life. In the background, the immortal Sun rises as an image of hope and resurrection between the two pillars, symbolizing life's duality.

Student *So what would you say to a person when Death comes up in a reading?*

Juliet Well, I would certainly not say it means death on a physical level. The Death card means that something in the person's life is ending, and this could be sad or a welcome relief, depending on their circumstances. There are so many

Alchemical prints show Cerberus (opposite) devouring flesh to prepare the work for its next stage.

The Medieval Scapini deck shows a dancing skeleton mowing a blue field of human heads and limbs. The hands and heads that lie on the ground are fresh, not decomposing, and, as such, do not represent the past, but rather the seeds of new life.

possible endings: the end of a relationship; the end of school; the end of a job; children leaving home; the end of single life with marriage – the list could go on and on!

The important thing to remember about Death is that the ending needs to be acknowledged, to be mourned and honoured, just as the Greeks honoured the process by paying the ferryman. Each event has a double-edge. For example, getting married is a happy step, yet it also requires mourning for the loss of freedom and youth that single life often affords. Equally, a divorce could bring the chance for freedom again, yet there needs to be mourning for the loss of the marriage. Whatever the circumstances, it is important to acknowledge the necessity for change and to honour the process fully.

Renewal through Dying

The Death card is a symbol of life that is renewed through the process of dying, and the alchemical parallel is the blackening, also called *nigredo* or 'putrefaction'. After coupling with the Queen, the King dies. The material in the alchemist's pot turns black and starts to stink, and the *nigredo* is heralded. This period of death and rotting is necessary to generate new life. 'No generation without corruption' was the maxim of the alchemist, and he welcomed the blackness of the putrefaction, knowing it must precede the whiteness, just as night precedes day. The corruption was generating new life within itself, just as the decay of autumn prepares the soil for new seeds in spring. Scorpio is the zodiac sign connected with transformation, death and rebirth. The Sun passes through this sign in November, when trees lose their leaves and plants die away before the decomposition process during the winter period, waiting for rejuvenation in the spring. The putrefaction can be likened psychologically to a period of melancholy or depression, symbolizing the spiritual rotting away of the old self, which can eventually give birth to a new one.

The alchemical texts depict the three-headed hound of Hell, Cerberus, devouring the subject of the work. The subject is stripped bare of all impurities, in the

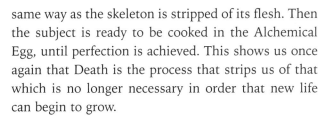

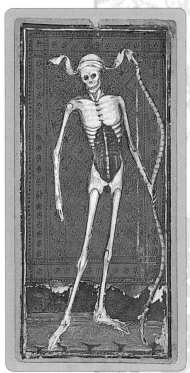

same way as the skeleton is stripped of its flesh. Then the subject is ready to be cooked in the Alchemical Egg, until perfection is achieved. This shows us once again that Death is the process that strips us of that which is no longer necessary in order that new life can begin to grow.

In the Visconti deck, a figure of a skeleton with the remnant of a shroud tied around its head stands at what appears to be the edge of a precipice.

◆ EXERCISE ◆

Examine your own views on death. It is a very emotive subject and one that can provoke fear and anxiety. How do you feel about it? Is it a subject that you prefer to ignore or can you allow yourself to think about it? Use the imagery on your tarot deck as a starting point for association. Consider the cycles in nature and in particular think about the season you are in, psychologically as well as literally, at the moment. Are you in a budding or a decaying phase?

Allow yourself to write, paint or sketch your own feelings about death. Think of all that has 'died' in your life, such as life stages you have passed or relationships that are gone. How did you feel about their passing at the time and how do you feel about them now?

TEMPERANCE

In alchemical texts, the image of the Peacock's Tail (see page 74) symbolizes the moment in the Great Work when a rainbow colouring is produced.

The Temperance card usually features an image of an angelic figure pouring liquid from one vessel into another. The Arthurian deck (*opposite*) differs from the norm by depicting a cauldron being stirred and tended by three women. Temperance, meaning 'to be moderate', is the fourth of the cardinal virtues.

Goddess of the Rainbow

The winged angel of the Temperance card has been identified with Iris, the goddess of the rainbow, who was Hera's special messenger, just as Hermes was Zeus'. In the same way as Hermes would guide the souls of dead men to the River Styx, so Iris would guide the souls of dead women. Iris was a gentle goddess, beloved by gods and mortals alike, and welcome everywhere: in Heaven, on Earth and in the underworld. She would descend to Earth using her rainbow as a bridge between the Heavens and the Earth. Even the gates to the underworld opened with ease when she visited to refill the golden cups of the Olympians with the immortal waters of the river Styx.

Water-carrier

The Temperance angel has also been identified with Ganymede, who became the cup-bearer to the immortals. The myth of Ganymede is also an example of humanity raised to divine status by the intercession of a god. Ganymede was an enchantingly beautiful youth with whom Zeus fell in love before carrying him off to Olympus, much to Hera's irritation. Hera was even more put out when Zeus gave Ganymede their daughter Hebe's position as cup-bearer to the gods. However, Zeus was amused at Hera's aggravation and set Ganymede's image in the constellation of Aquarius to annoy her even more.

xiv the cauldron

In Egyptian myth, Temperance has been linked with Hapi, the god of the Nile, whose waters were seen as source of both agricultural and spiritual life. In the Egyptian zodiac, Aquarius is shown as carrying two containers rather than one.

Promise of New Life

The symbolism in this card is very rich. The Arthurian deck (*left*) features a cauldron which, according to Celtic myth, could never be emptied and therefore no one would ever remain unnourished. It was said that the liquid even had the power to bring the dead to life. The cauldron can be connected with the Grail itself, for it gives wisdom, heals wounds and brings everlasting life.

The golden irises growing next to the water on the Waite card (*right*) symbolize the goddess of the rainbow. A rainbow was sent by God after Noah's flood as a promise that He would not destroy the world by water again. It is therefore regarded as a symbol of peace and reconciliation and, as Temperance follows Death, the rainbow can be seen as the promise of new life. In the background, the Sun is rising over twin mountain peaks, an image of a new dawn. In this card, the man-made pillars, which so often represent duality in the tarot, have been replaced by natural stones, to denote that Temperance is an instinctual card.

The Waite deck shows the angel standing beside a pool with one foot in the water and one on the rocks, to symbolize continuity between past and future. The angel himself represents the present, which mediates between the two.

In the Arthurian deck, three women tend the cauldron, which may refer to the three stages of life – youth, maturity and old age – and the three phases of the Moon.

TEMPERANCE.

Moderation in All Things

The theme of Temperance is moderation; nothing should exist in extreme. If something is too dry, it should be moistened; if it is too wet, it should be dried. Nothing should be too hot, nor too cold.

Temperance, as one of the cardinal virtues, may depict the custom of diluting wine with water to moderate the effect of the alcohol, and may also allude to the mixing of water with wine during the Christian communion ceremony, which mixes the water of man with the blood of Christ, which he sacrificed to redeem humanity.

Blending of Opposites

In the Medieval Scapini deck (*below*), the water-carrying angel uses vessels made in the shape of a crescent Moon and a lion, representing the Sun. This action symbolizes the blending of opposites, such as feminine and masculine, passive and active, dark and light.

The alchemical process is central to the card of Temperance because it involved a continual focus on keeping the work in a state of unity and separation. After the *nigredo*, as seen in the Death card, the next stage to arrive was the appearance of a rainbow, leading the alchemist to believe he was on the right track. Iris (*see page 72*) is the harbinger of death for women. In alchemy, in order to release women's souls it was necessary to sublime the volatile parts of the residue left after the *nigredo*. This would produce a rainbow colouring that was known as the Peacock's Tail. The combination of water, which is feminine, and Sun, which is masculine, creates a rainbow: an image of the successful union of opposites.

On the right-hand side of the Medieval Scapini card is a tiny scene depicting John the Baptist baptizing Christ while the dove of the Holy Ghost descends. The angel's face has been modelled on paintings of John the Baptist by Leonardo da Vinci.

◇ **Student** *I think this is a beautiful card, which makes me feel calm. Is it a 'feeling' card?*

◇ Juliet Yes, it is. In the way that Justice (an 'Air' or 'intellect' card) requires a balanced mind, so Temperance (a 'Water' or 'feeling' card) requires a balanced heart. In order to keep the feelings balanced, they must be allowed to move, mix and blend constantly, because water that is allowed to stay still eventually stagnates and becomes toxic. So, the image of the angel pouring water from one cup to another, very carefully and in a measured way, signifies the need for continual movement of feelings, both between the people involved in relationships and internally between conscious and unconscious. The Temperance card carries the divinatory meaning of a harmonious and successful relationship, which is achieved when the persons involved are prepared to compromise and cooperate, to blend with one another and not be too rigid.

When Temperance appears in a reading, the time is ripe for discussion, for sharing feelings rather than repressing them. It indicates that revelation rather than keeping one's own counsel is the order of the day.

• EXERCISE •

To experiment with the idea of mixing and blending, let yourself loose in the kitchen. This is an opportunity to experiment with mixing opposites, such as flour and water. In order to make a supple paste that can be kneaded and shaped, it is necessary to add the ingredients with care. If you add too much liquid, you must compensate with more powder until you achieve a balanced solution. You can do the same with any ingredients you feel moved to 'play' with.

Now turn your attention to your inner world and notice how difficult, or otherwise, it is for you to keep your emotions balanced. For example, how difficult is it for you to feel ambivalent about something or someone? Can you allow yourself to both love and hate the same person at the same time without letting one emotion supplant the other? How do your active and passive feelings coexist within? Use the image of Temperance to focus on these issues and, as always, make notes of your findings.

The Renaissance Tarot image has something of the quality of the sign Aquarius, the water-carrier, with the figure of a beautiful angel pouring water from one jug to another.

Blocks that hinder
growth can be removed
and energy released

THE DEVIL

XV·IL DIAVOLO·THE DEVIL·ۨ

*The Renaissance deck
shows Pan as The Devil.
He is in light-hearted mood
as a dejected couple sit
chained at his feet.*

$\mathbf{M}$ost decks depict The Devil as a half-human, half-goat figure, often standing on a square pedestal, which symbolizes matter and may be a reference to the throne of The Emperor. A man and a woman are generally attached by their necks to the pedestal. The Devil usually has the wings of a bat and little horns on his head, but his hands are human. He has female breasts to show that he is not wholly masculine. Like Death, The Devil is a card that often evokes fear in those who are unfamiliar with it, as its image is of a very powerful archetypal energy.

God of Untamed Nature

The representation of a goat-like figure holding two figures captive immediately brings to mind Satan, the Christian devil. In fact, as you can see in the Renaissance deck (*above*), the classical image of The Devil is very like that of the Greek goat-god Pan, who was so ugly that even his own mother ran away from him in horror. Shunned by polite society, Pan lived alone in the pastures of Arcadia as the god of untamed nature and sexuality, where he was responsible for the fertility of herds and flocks. His powerful desire was legendary, and he was most famous for his hot pursuit of the nymph Syrinx, who threw herself into a river rather than submit to his advances. When she changed herself into a clump of reeds, Pan chopped them down and made them into pan-pipes. He called the instrument he had made a syrinx and played wonderful tunes on it.

Pan was despised by the Olympian gods, who found him too coarse and brutish for their civilized taste, but they were not above exploiting his powers. Apollo, the Sun-god, coaxed the art of prophecy from him, while Hermes copied one of his pipes, claimed it as his own idea and promptly sold it to his brother, Apollo. Pan was the only Greek god to have been officially declared dead. Plutarch recounts that a mariner sailing near the Echinades Islands heard a mysterious voice call out three times saying, 'When you reach Palodes, proclaim that the great god Pan is dead.' At the same time, Christianity was born in Judea. Christians abhorred the desires of the flesh, and for a long time declared that sexuality was synonymous with evil, embodied in the lustful image of Pan, who was relegated to hell.

Your Shadow Side

In psychological terms, The Devil represents the shadow side of the personality. It is the part of the personality that we are least proud of, least want to own and would rather leave buried in the depths of the psyche – just as we buried Satan deep in the bowels of the Earth. The shadow is first glimpsed by The Fool in the shape of the wild horses of The Chariot and the powerful lion of Strength. However, while these images seem quite acceptable – even noble and majestic – the image of The Devil does not. He is ugly, greedy and lustful, and the figure on the Visconti deck (*below*) accentuates this point by featuring elements of both goat and ass.

The Devil embodies everything the last 2,000 years of civilization has taught us to despise. The shadow is that side of the personality that carries our fear and self-loathing and, like the figures chained to The Devil, holds us captive through that fear and disgust. Yet, if The Devil can be brought to consciousness in a measured manner, the darkness can become light. The seeds of life lie in the dark, and Satan can become Lucifer, whose name means 'bringer of light'.

In the Visconti deck, a figure with the body of a man, female breasts and the hind legs of a goat stands on a pedestal. He has the horns of a goat and the ears of an ass, both animals being connected with lust and sexuality.

Student *So this devil has nothing to do with Black Magic or Satanism?*

Juliet No. In the tarot, The Devil represents the dark side of ourselves, which is not evil, only dark. Anything dark or unknown makes us fearful. So the task that The Devil offers us is to make known the unconscious side so it can be worked with rather than repressed. The divinatory meaning

The lusty goat-god (right) is shown holding his famous pan-pipes to his lips.

of this card is 'greater power and energy if blocks or inhibitions can be released'. Pan is linked with animal desire, lust for life and huge energy, which can enrich the personality when they are confronted rather than repressed.

In many decks, The Devil has two figures in attendance: a man and a woman who are attached or chained to him, yet with their hands free. This indicates that they are held captive to The Devil – who symbolizes, in this instance, the material – through their own choice. If they wished, they could use their hands to free themselves.

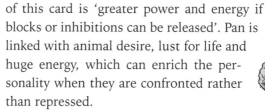

On the Wirth card, The Devil has a female form yet the face of a goat. All four elements are featured: his wings represent Air; he carries a flame, symbolizing Fire; the fish-like scales on his legs represent Water; and the green, female goat symbolizes Earth.

The image of the goat has another function, that of 'scapegoat', which is an object onto which we can project our own unpleasantness to make ourselves feel better. In this way, we often blame The Devil for everything that goes wrong in our lives. This is easier than looking deep within ourselves to see what part we have played in our misfortune.

Dissolve and Coagulate

The work of the alchemists involved achieving a perfect balance. Part of their painstaking work was a constant process of separation and reunion; purification and regeneration, following putrefaction. Likewise, the desire described by The Devil should neither be repressed nor should it be allowed to overtake the personality completely, rather it should be balanced. On the Wirth deck (*left*), the words engraved on the Devil's arm read 'solve' and 'coagula', which is the universal alchemical formula, meaning 'dissolve and coagulate'. In the words of the legendary Egyptian philosopher, Hermes Trismegistus: 'It rises from the Earth to the sky (*solve*) and again

descends into the Earth (*coagula*) and receives the force of things superior and inferior … if you dissolve the fixed, and make fixed the volatile, and make fast the winged thing, it will make you live safely.'

Fallen Angel

In most tarot images, The Devil has bat-like wings which may be a Christian addition, as Satan was, at one time, an angel. It seems that good angels had feathery wings and bad ones had leathery ones. According to the Wirth (*opposite page*) and Medieval Scapini (*right*) decks, The Devil's wings and the star on his forehead indicate that he was once Lucifer. He carries a sword without a hilt, to symbolize unleashed sexuality. His horns or antlers have connected him with an ancient Celtic stag-god Cernunnos, who was an underworld deity.

In the Medieval Scapini deck, a captive couple dance the sensual tango and are attached to The Devil with a golden chain, a symbol of earthly wealth.

• EXERCISE •

Sit down with The Devil card and contemplate the imagery carefully. How do you feel about this card? Allow all your spontaneous associations to come to the surface and make notes of your thoughts. What is your attitude to the stuff of the Devil? How easy is it for you to face your shadow self? Are you aware of what your shadow personality is composed of?

It is very difficult to uncover the truths of this card because it deals with the unconscious which is, by its very nature, unknown to you consciously. One way of getting close to your unconscious is to think of all the things you most hate in others and then see how many of them apply to yourself! For example, if you loathe lazy people, there may be a strong element of laziness lying repressed within you! It is not easy to confront yourself with the truth, but it is a worthwhile exercise if you can do it periodically.

Breaking down existing
structures to make way
for the new • Catharsis
Clearing ways

THE TOWER

XVI

The Falling Tower

*The Tower in the Scapini
deck represents Babel, built
on sand, meaning it is not
a solid foundation, with
seven storeys, one for each
of the seven deadly sins.*

The traditional imagery of this card is lightning
crashing into a tall tower, cracking its structure
and throwing its occupants out with considerable
force. It is a violent and dramatic image in which a
carefully constructed and preserved building is shattered by the enormous power of nature. It marks the
last stage of The Fool's underworld journey before the
arrival of the dawn in The Star (*see page 84*).

There are a number of possible mythic interpretations to this card. Its French title in the Wirth deck (*see
page 83*) is 'La Maison Dieu', which has led many inter-
preters to believe it is the House of God that is being
shattered. However, according to Paul Huson, in *The
Devil's Picturebook*, much older decks give this card the
title 'La Maison Diefel', meaning 'House of the Devil'.
So it seems that The Tower might actually represent
Hell, which is being split open by divine light.

Fall of the Arrogant

Many writers on the tarot have connected this image with the Tower
of Babel, which was built by Noah's descendants, who were annoyed
with God for having flooded the world. They wished to take issue on
this subject with God and so attempted to construct a fabulously tall
tower, high enough so they could use it to reach heaven and argue
with God. Of course, they failed miserably and not only was the tower
destroyed, but God made each of them speak different languages, so
they could no longer communicate with one another.

There is a clear message about arrogance in this card, and the
Mythic Tarot (*opposite*) uses a Greek myth to further illustrate the
point. Minos of Crete made a deal with the god Poseidon that, should
the god make him king, he would sacrifice a beautiful white bull in
honour of the god. Poseidon kept his side of the bargain but King
Minos did not. He foolishly substituted an inferior bull for the sacri-

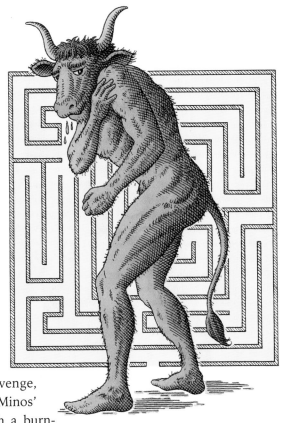

In the Mythic Tarot, the ocean god Poseidon rises up from the waves, lightning flashing from his trident. The four natural elements are present in the rocks, sea, clouds and lightning.

fice, and, in revenge, Poseidon inflicted Minos' wife, Pasiphae, with a burning desire for the white bull. The result of this strange union was the Minotaur, a fearsome creature, half-man half-bull, which fed exclusively on virgin human flesh. The humiliated king ordered a labyrinth to be built to house this shameful creature, unwilling to acknowledge that it was his own deceit and greed that was ultimately responsible for its birth. Eventually, the hero Theseus killed the beast and Poseidon destroyed the labyrinth once it no longer served any purpose.

Rebirth of Dionysus

Yet another way of looking at this card is through the lens of the Mystery Plays (*see page 13*). This card marks the freedom of Dionysus from death and his rebirth as the god of light. There are two versions of the story of

THE TOWER

Dionysus' rebirth, both of which are accompanied by divine fire. In one version, Dionysus is the son of Zeus and Semele, a mortal woman, whom Hera destroys by divine fire. Zeus manages to save the unborn child by sewing the foetus up in his thigh until it is time for the delivery of the baby. In the second version, the wicked Titans destroy Dionysus, and Zeus, in turn, uses divine fire to destroy them, while saving the heart of his child and feeding it to Persephone in the form of pomegranate seeds. In this way, Dionysus becomes the god of light, born to the Queen of the Underworld. The dark underworld womb carries the seeds of life and is split open by divine lightning.

Put another way, the Sun descends to its lowest point at the time of the winter solstice, after which it starts to increase in strength again, thus defeating winter and the powers of darkness.

The Renaissance deck shows The Tower to be that of Babel, with tiny images of Phaëton and Icarus in the corners. They both flew too near to the Sun and so, along with Babel, represent hubris, which is a Greek term for arrogance in the face of the gods.

Student *So how would you interpret The Tower in a reading?*

Juliet The Tower marks a point in life when a person must seriously consider their external world, their beliefs and their worldly point of view, which may be in need of an overhaul. The Tower usually suggests that something in a person's life has become too rigid and restricting and there is need for change and growth. But, because of the rigidity and inflexibility of the structures, there is no room for expansion, so the structure must first be shattered. As the Tower is a man-made structure, this card is to do with what society expects of us. With Death and The Devil, the issues are intensely personal, indicating a painful confrontation with the inner world. With The Tower, however, the way a person actually lives his or her external life is under scrutiny and involves the prospect of change. Before new ways of living can be set in motion, though, the old must be dismantled.

Violent Change

The symbolism and imagery on this card are clear: no matter how strong and impressive man-made constructs are, they are always subject explicitly to the forces of nature and implicitly to the will of God. As is apparent from the Wirth deck (*right*), the figures tumbling from The Tower are helpless, as the falling debris strikes them down.

XVI

la Maison Dieu Y

The Tower is the only card that uses a structure for its subject; all the other cards use planets or figures, human or godlike, as their symbols. This structure represents society and The Tower signifies that The Fool must carefully examine society's laws and rules to see whether they are truly meaningful to him or whether they no longer have the relevance they once had. The walls must be torn down, just as the lightning of truth and enlightenment strike the top of The Tower. The only certainty in life is change, and this violent image suggests that, if we allow ourselves to become rigid and inflexible, the change will be more painful than if we learn to adapt to the prevailing circumstances and move with the times.

• EXERCISE •

Look at the image on this card and call to mind a time in your life when a cataclysmic event shattered and changed your life. This might be an experience such as moving house, changing jobs, being made redundant or leaving school, or a personal trauma, such as the end of an important friendship or relationship. With the benefit of hindsight can you see how this had to happen? Can you feel the positive effect? Do you concentrate on the release or the tension?

Consider your own point of view regarding change. Is it easy or difficult for you? Consider your values now and those of your parents when you were a child. Have you held on to the values of your upbringing or have you changed your views? Do you prefer to hold on to things whether they are useful or not, or can you let go? As always, make notes about your thoughts on this card.

The crowned figure in the Wirth deck wears the colours of the four elements: red for Fire, yellow for Air, green for Earth and blue for Water. The lightning represents the divine fire that is essential for the alchemical work to take place.

THE STAR

XVII • LE STELLE • THE STARS

In the top left corner of the Renaissance card is the nymph Astraea, who lived on Earth when men were gentle. As soon as they became more aggressive and warlike, she retired to the heavens in the constellation of Virgo. The swan, her familiar, is in the top right corner.

The image of the young woman pouring water from a jug or jugs under a starry sky presents a peaceful change after the heaviness of Death, The Devil and The Tower. She represents the calm after the storm; the welcome dawn after the darkest hour.

There are a number of possibilities surrounding the origin of The Star maiden. Like the Temperance angel (*see page 72*), she has been connected with Ganymede and Hebe, cup-bearers to the Olympians. She has also been linked with Aphrodite, who had the brightest star known to the ancients: the planet Venus. This planet made two appearances each night, one just after sunset and the other just before dawn. She was thought to shine out to those who were in the greatest darkness. The title of Morning Star, or Phosphorus Aster, was given to Iacchus, the reborn Dionysus (*see page 19*).

The Star can also be connected with the Egyptian goddess Isis, whose magical star would appear each year immediately before the arrival of the welcome rains. The river Nile represented life to the people of Egypt and it seemed to them that the Star of Isis appeared each year to announce that the rains would come in time to save them from drought and starvation. So, to them, The Star was a symbol of promise.

Life, Death and Rebirth

The Star maiden has also been connected with Inanna, the Sumerian goddess of love and fertility. Her eight-pointed star, as presented in ancient drawings, is featured on many early decks. Inana was an earth goddess married to a shepherd named Dumuzi, and many pairs of temples were dedicated to their joint worship. Each year the king of the city would impersonate Dumuzi, and the high priestess would impersonate Inana herself, in an annual marriage ceremony that was intended to secure prosperity and fertility to the land.

The goddess Inana's descent into the underworld is the oldest version of the universal myth of souls journeying from the land of the living to the land of the dead. Inana had a strong wish to visit her sister Ereshkigal, 'the mistress of death', who lived beneath the earth in the 'land of no return'. Although all warned her against it, Inana was determined to visit this place and return. Undaunted, she descended and was duly sentenced to death by her sister, who hung her on a hook where, like a piece of rotting meat, she turned green with decay. Fortunately Inana's handmaiden managed to save her, and she was finally allowed to go back to the land of the living provided she sent someone to take her place in the 'land of no return'. She agreed to this demand. When she arrived home, to her intense irritation she discovered her husband Dumuzi enjoying himself immensely. Annoyed that he was not wearing sackcloth and mourning her loss, she declared that he would be the one to take her place. After a while she softened a little and allowed her other sister to serve six months of the year in Dumuzi's place.

The theme of this myth – that is of life, death and rebirth – is echoed in all cultures. It appears in the stories of Demeter and Persephone, Osiris and Horus, and of course as the reborn hero Dionysus, who conquered the powers of darkness and was duly returned to the light.

The young woman on the Visconti card gazes up at an eight-pointed star. She stands between two mountain peaks, symbolizing balance between opposites.

Guiding Light

The Star has always been a symbol of hope and an essential light to guide wayfarers and mariners. The Three Wise Men in the Bible followed the bright star to Bethlehem, where the 'Light of the World' would be born. The maiden on The Star is young and naked, because she represents renewal and the truth revealed. She pours the waters of life freely, sometimes from two jugs – one silver, one gold – representing the Moon and the Sun united. When she uses two jugs, one pours water into a pool, which symbolizes the unconscious, and the other pours water over the land, the conscious mind. This reminds us that

Old alchemical imagery
shows the Quintessence as
a young woman crowned
with stars, standing
between the Sun and the
Moon. The Quintessence
was the ethereal substance
that held the four elements
in perfect suspension.

The Morgan Greer deck
shows the maiden in a
landscape containing the
four elements: Water in the
pool, the bird symbolizing
Air; trees and flowers representing Earth; and stars
symbolizing divine Fire.

insight is available to both unconscious and conscious alike. The liquid is not measured or poured carefully as it is in the Temperance card. It flows freely, suggesting that the time for restrictions is over.

Behind the woman on the Morgan Greer card (*left*), an ibis sits on a tree. This was the sacred bird of Egyptian Thoth, god of wisdom, and is a symbol of the soul's ability to rise to higher levels. In the Wirth deck (*opposite right*), a butterfly perches on a red flower, which represents the soul's numerous stages of transformation.

The alchemists believed the star was a symbol for the imagination. After the darkness of the *nigredo* comes the light of rebirth and the promise that alchemical gold is in sight.

Star of Hope

Many decks depict eight stars: one large, often eight-pointed, star in the centre, surrounded by seven smaller ones. In addition to its connection with Inana, the eight-pointed star is also linked with baptism, because

XVII — THE STAR

eight is the number of rebirth. The Fool has received his trial by fire in The Tower and is now ready to be quenched by the healing waters of The Star. The seven small stars might represent the Pleiades, who were seven sisters, daughters of Atlas. Orion, the hunter, caught sight of the beautiful girls and pursued them. They cried out to Zeus to save them and he turned them into a flock of doves so they could fly away. Later he turned them into seven stars, the constellation of the Pleiades, so they came to symbolize immortality.

Student *So in a reading this card would represent hope and inspiration?*

Juliet Yes, it is in many ways one of the nicest cards in the deck because it suggests that no matter how dark and difficult life is at the moment, there is always hope for the future. It has an optimistic feel to it, which gives one the strength to carry on even when life looks bleak.

• EXERCISE •

Concentrate on the image on The Star card. Think about what The Star means to you personally. Try to think of a time when you desperately needed hope and how you found it. Think about the feelings evoked by The Star. Go outside on a clear night and look up at the stars. Take time to be alone in the darkness with only the stars for light. How does that make you feel? Write down everything that is connected with the night and those pinpoints of light up in the sky.

Think of all the connections with stars that you can – wishing upon stars, lucky stars, stars of wonder, stars that guide and direct. Find a special piece of music that might summon up emotions connected with this hopeful and inspiring card.

The Wirth deck shows the young girl pouring water into the Pool of Memory, which lies on the edge of the underworld. Those returning from the land of the dead would drink from this pool, so they might not forget their mystical experience.

THE MOON

The Moon card generally shows a pool in the foreground with a crab or crayfish crawling out of it, while dogs bark at the Full Moon overhead. In the distance, a path leads between two pillars or towers. The scene has an eerie quality.

The Three Faces of the Moon

The Moon is the ancient ruler of the night and is connected in Greek myth with Artemis, the virgin huntress. The Moon has three phases and three associated faces: the crescent Moon, the Full Moon and the Dark Moon. She was regarded by the ancients as one Great Goddess with Many Names. The crescent new Moon represents the Virgin, and is associated with the virgin goddesses, such as Athene (*see page 49*), Artemis and Persephone (*see page 25*). The Full Moon is the virgin fulfilled – the Great Mother – and is connected with the fertility goddesses, such as Demeter (*see page 29*) and Isis (*see pages 18 and 84*). The Dark Moon is the Old Woman or the Hag, and is associated with such dark goddesses as Ereshkigal, the Sumerian goddess of the 'land of no return' (*see page 85*) and Hecate, Greek goddess of the underworld.

Hecate, which means 'the distant one', had authority over the fertility of the earth and the hours of darkness. She could bestow wealth, success and good luck if it pleased her to do so; yet she could also show a much less generous aspect. She could appear entwined with snakes, as the keeper of the keys of the underworld, and would torment men through their dreams. Haunting crossroads and graveyards, she was mistress of magic and enchantment. This dark aspect of the Moon is often hinted at in The Moon card.

Medusa, the snake-haired Gorgon, can also be linked with the dark aspect of the Moon. Medusa, who was once extremely beautiful, committed the crime of coupling with the ocean god Poseidon in the virgin

The Mythic Tarot shows the triple-headed goddess, Hecate, crowned with the Moon's phases. By her side is her triple-headed dog, which sees past, present and future. The crab emerging from the pool is the symbol of the astrological sign of Cancer.

THE MOON

goddess Athene's sacred temple. The goddess was enraged and punished Medusa by making her face so terrifying that any mortal who looked at her would instantly turn to stone. Athene later helped the hero Perseus to behead Medusa by providing him with a silver shield, in which he could see the reflection of the Gorgon. In this way Perseus could be sure of his aim without having to look at Medusa directly, thus avoiding simultaneously being turned to stone. Silver and reflecting objects are all associated with lunar magic. Medusa's severed head was shared between Persephone and Athene. Persephone set the head in the underworld, and Athene had its image engraved on her silver sword, perhaps to symbolize that new life and death are inseparable.

The head of Medusa (left) provides decoration for Persephone's underworld throne.

The Wirth deck shows a deep pool, perhaps the Pool of Forgetfulness, which lies near the Pool of Memory in the underworld. It is said that each soul drinks from its waters before starting a new life.

Femininity and Fertility

The Moon was observed by the ancients to govern the flow of the tides and was seen to rule the waxing and waning rhythms of life. The living tide – the flow of blood in the female menstrual cycle – was also seen to coincide with the twenty-eight days of the Moon's cycle from new, to full, to old. The Moon, the mistress of night, was also seen by the ancients as the womb from which new life sprang each day and the tomb to which all returned each night to rest, sleep and dream. She represented all aspects of the Great Mother: the promise of a fertile womb, the fulfilment of that promise in maturity, and the return to her in death.

The analogy of the Moon as the womb is an apt one. During a pregnancy, the gestation period when a foetus is shaped is vital, yet throughout that time no one can see the growth of the embryo. Only at the moment of delivery does it become clear what has been gestating in secret. This is also true of the creative ideas that gestate in the unconscious and do not become formed until the moment of birth.

The Creativity of the Unconscious

What is seen by moonlight can look very different by the clear light of day. This is why The Moon card is often interpreted as deceptive or sinister. The Moon presides over the unconscious, the place from which dreams and fantasies spring spontaneously, and it is difficult to explain what she reveals in a logical or conceptual way. She is the queen of creativity but her realm is different from the bright creativity of her brother, The Sun. She provides the fragile threads of notions and ideas, which, when brought to the light, can take shape and form.

The animals barking at the Moon in The Moon card of most tarot decks are often represented as a dog and a wolf, and symbolize the animal side of man. The crab or crayfish that emerges from the water represents the primitive notions that arise from the collective unconscious and the deep imagination. The road winding between two pillars or towers is the 'royal road' of dreams. The creature from the deep emerges to give us a glimpse of what is in the unconscious, and then slips quietly back into the deep water. This can happen, too, with dreams: the story and meaning seem so clear at the time of dreaming but slip away on waking.

The Morgan Greer deck shows a deep pool with a crayfish crawling out of it, symbolizing the process of birth. A wolf and a dog bay at the Full Moon.

XVIII — THE MOON

Student *So how do you interpret such a confusing card in a reading?*

Juliet In a reading, The Moon reflects a time of confusion in the seeker's life, which I would say needs to be allowed rather than avoided. We often wish to soften the pain and panic of confusion by finding answers and solutions. However, if The Moon appears in a reading, it means that whatever the confusion is about it is still being 'gestated' and must, therefore, be left to work itself out. The Moon is a creative card but its creativity needs to be allowed to evolve gradually and should not be forced. The mood swings often associated with this card need to be allowed too; they will pass, but in their own time.

This card is not dissimilar to The High Priestess, although The Moon feels a little darker and perhaps concentrates on the endings of matters rather than on new potential, as in The High Priestess.

Certainties Dissolved

The parallel this card has with alchemy is probably in the process called 'solution', in which the material in the alchemist's vessel is dissolved into a watery state. Psychologically speaking, this marks the stage of self-criticism and self-doubt in which previously held certainties and truths are slowly dissolved in what the alchemists described as an 'ordeal by bitter water'. The two bodies become one as they slowly dissolve into the liquid state.

XVIII · LA LVNA · THE MOON

The Renaissance Tarot shows a huge Moon under which two maidens make music, a symbol of the creative potential of this card. In the top right-hand corner is the Moon goddess, Artemis the huntress, and in the other corner the hunted stag.

◆ EXERCISE ◆

To get to know the essence of The Moon there is nothing better than watching her make her monthly night-time transformation from new to full to old. As you observe her cyclical changes, notice how you feel during each of her phases. Look at your tarot image and allow your mind to wander, using the picture as a starting point. Perhaps you can find a piece of music, or a lunar perfume such as jasmine, to associate with The Moon. Collect lunar metals, flowers and fruits, such as silver, mirrors, lilies, white roses and pomegranates, and make a lunar display. You could also include water or water lilies. Allow your artistic instincts and your imagination free rein!

THE SUN

THE SUN

In the distance on the Mythic Tarot card stands a pair of laurel trees, sacred to Apollo, whose leaves were used to crown the winners of artistic or athletic contests.

In most decks, the image of a brightly shining Sun is vividly depicted in The Sun card. Usually it takes the form of a luminous face, sometimes carried by a naked child, who is often shown riding a white horse.

Connections with Sun Gods

The Sun card has obvious links with solar gods, such as Helios, who drove the golden chariot that carried the sun and was pulled by magnificent white horses. The Iranian sun-god, Mithra, drove a similar horse-drawn chariot. Mithra was known as *sol invictus*, 'the unconquered sun', and his victory over darkness was seen as a promise that man will be reborn. The Sun is also connected with Hyperion, a Titan, whose name means 'dweller on high'. Hyperion married his sister Theia, and together they produced Helios and Selene, the early Sun and Moon gods. Often regarded as siblings or twins, the sun and moon represent two sides of the same coin, each presiding over a portion of the twenty-four-hour period.

Children of the great Zeus and Leto, Apollo and his twin sister Artemis, were second-generation Olympians, who replaced Helios and Selene as guardians of the Sun and Moon. Apollo was nicknamed Phoebus, which means 'the brilliant', and he was the beautiful god of art, literature and music, as shown in the Mythic Tarot (*above*). He was also a healer. It was believed that if sorrows and fears were put into an art form, such as a song, poem or painting, Apollo would take the grief away. Apollo also possessed the gift of prophecy, and many came to his oracle at Delphi for advice. Every autumn he left Delphi for the mysterious land of the Hyperboreans, who were a supremely happy people. He was their high god and went to them at set times of the year to receive their homage. When he returned to Delphi in mid-summer, nature would cover herself in flowers so that she would be at her most beautiful to receive him.

The Sun's Annual Cycle

The solar journey echoes the familiar theme in the tarot of death and rebirth. The sun's birthday is the winter solstice which, in the northern hemisphere, coincides with the date chosen by the Christians to celebrate the birth of Christ as the Son of Righteousness and the lord and giver of life. At the winter solstice the Sun's rays are at their weakest, representing the dying god, soon to be reborn as a child. Mistletoe was a solar plant associated with the Norse god, Balder, while bay was Apollo's sacred planet. Both plants were thought to be useful in fighting evil, and they were used for decoration at the winter solstice to help the Sun in its struggle with the powers of darkness.

In midsummer, when the sun is strong, it was seen by the ancients as the mighty celestial ruler at the prime of life and strength. The Sun's passage through the seasons, from blossom to fruit to decay and finally to death, reflects life's journey through youth, maturity and old age. The white horse on which the children ride on The Sun card of the Medieval Scapini (*see page 94*) and the Waite (*see page 95*) decks could be the same one as that ridden by Death on the Waite card (*see page 69*).

Warmth and Optimism

The Sun in the tarot may be associated with the phase in the alchemical process when the Sun King and the Moon Queen are joined in passion. The red and gold flames of the alchemist's fire reflect solar colours. The fixed Philosophic Sulphur and the volatile Philosophic Mercury unite, the matter dries out and is transformed into a bright red powder. This phase is called the *rubedo*, or reddening. It is from this red heat that their child, the Philosopher's Stone, is conceived. It is the welcome reward after a long period of waiting and watching through the *nigredo* (*see page 12*), like the appearance of the Sun after a cold night.

The imagery of The Sun card is essentially a beneficent one. The smiling children may be seen as opposites united, as well as symbols of joy, innocence,

The figure in the Visconti deck wears a twelve-stone necklace to represent the twelve signs of the zodiac through which the Sun makes its annual journey.

The 'blood of the green lion' (right) in alchemical lore, is the Hermetic Mercury, which is disgorged together with the sun, the Sulphur of the Wise.

sincerity and freedom. The theme of the red banner draped around or waved by the figures is a symbol of triumph and achievement. The two children that are depicted on the Medieval Scapini deck (*below*) may be identified with Castor and Pollux, the heavenly twins whose stars traditionally helped seafarers to find their way home. Because one twin was mortal and the other divine and they wished never to be parted, they lived alternately in the underworld and on Olympus, an image of opposites united. And Zeus placed their twin stars in the constellation of Gemini.

In the bottom right-hand corner of the Medieval Scapini card is an opened egg, representing the egg from which the heavenly twins were hatched.

Respect the Power

There are also warnings in myths related to the Sun – Icarus flew too close to the Sun, which melted his wax wings, and Phaëton arrogantly tried to drive the Sun chariot (*see page 46*). They both fell to their deaths, reminding us that The Sun is bright and brilliant but needs to be approached with respect, not arrogance.

The Sun in the Waite deck (*oposite page*) shows the Sun's rays to be alternately straight and wavy, signifying the positive and negative functions of the Sun. Positively, the Sun can ripen, bring to fruition, heal and enlighten; negatively, it can scorch, parch, shrivel crops and ultimately kill. In cool climates, the Sun is welcomed as a bringer of health and warmth, while in hotter countries it can be seen as the destroyer of life. In the Medieval Scapini (*left*) and Waite (*opposite page*)

XVIIII

The Sun

decks, a boundary wall can be seen. This represents structure and limitation: the Sun must follow a particular route on its annual journey around the circle of the zodiac; it cannot break from its natural bounds. It also hints at the importance of self-control.

Student *How does that impact on the divinatory meaning of The Sun?*

Juliet The Sun is relatively easy to interpret. It suggests a time of optimism, cheerfulness and enthusiasm, as the Sun's fiery rays bring elation. But remember the wall! It represents the limit within which one must keep. Otherwise The Sun may prove destructive, parching crops and drying rivers, killing our source of life. The Sun and Moon cards teach us that we need both in equal proportions.

• EXERCISE •

Observe the Sun at its most potent hours: dawn, midday and sunset. Notice how each time of day has a very different feel. Mediate on The Sun card image at each of these different times and notice what effect this has on your feeling about the image. Make notes on your reflections. Notice whether your mood changes when the sun is shining. St John's Wort, a recently 'rediscovered' herbal remedy for depression and low spirits, was thought of by the medieval herbalist as good for evoking 'solar' virtues, such as cheerfulness and optimism. Find a rousing piece of music that inspires enthusiasm in you. Collect metals, plants, flowers and fruits associated with the Sun, such as gold, brass, laurel, bay, sunflowers, heliotrope and oranges, and make a display. You could add candles as a symbol of solar fire. Experiment with the notion of offering your sorrows to Apollo through works of art – you may be surprised at how effectively it works!

The Waite deck shows sunflowers peeking over the wall. These are solar flowers, both due to their appearance and because their heads follow the Sun.

JUDGEMENT

XX — JUDGMENT

The image on the Judgement card in most tarot decks calls to mind the legendary Day of Judgement. Graves open and bodies emerge to the sound of the trumpet blast from a heavenly creature. This card is also called Resurrection or The Angel.

The image of the dead being called to rise, as depicted in most decks, is what was anticipated would happen on the day the world came to an end. On this day St Michael, the archangel, would sound the trumpet, which would be loud enough to waken the dead and bring them from their graves, their hands clasped in prayer. They would then be judged by God, the angels and the saints, who would weigh the evidence for good and bad according to the deeds they had performed throughout their lives. On receiving the final judgement, they would be duly dispatched to Heaven or Hell.

In the distance on the Morgan Greer card are mountains and above, from the clouds, emerges a trumpet surrounded in flames. These point to the four elements, and the three figures represent the three parts of mankind: mind, body and spirit.

Guide of Souls After Death

The angel whose duty it was to wake the dead – St Michael – was also the Christian guide of souls after death and the leader of the forces of good and light over those of evil and dark during the war of Heaven between God and Satan. Many authors have identified Michael with Hermes Psychopomp, the classical guide of souls, whose task it was to lay his golden staff upon the eyes of the dying and usher them gently into Hades' realm. He could also, in certain circumstances, lead the dead back out of the underworld. Hermes began the journey through the tarot trumps in the form of the Magician, so it seems fitting that he should close the circle at the end as Angel of the Dead. According to the Hebrew Cabbala, Michael was one of the seven mighty archangels who guided the planets in their courses, and the planet Mercury, Hermes to the Greeks, came under his influence.

It would appear that, like Michael, many Christian angels and saints took over the duties of pagan deities with only a change of name and symbol so that they could fit in with the new religion. The gods of older religions often became the devils of the new, which is why the tarot, with so many images of pagan deities, was referred to by the Puritans, who vigorously denounced it, as 'the devil's picturebook'.

Reaping What You Sow

The Judgement card is an image of new life conquering the darkness of the grave. Jesus said that unless a grain of wheat were to fall onto the earth and die, it would remain alone and barren. But if it were to die it would bear much fruit. He continued (John 12.24–5): 'He who loves his life loses it, and he who hates his life in this world will keep it for eternal life.' Most decks use three figures – man, woman and child – as the rising dead, perhaps as a hint that at any stage of life, youth, maturity or old age, the moment of judgement can present itself to us. The notion of judgement is similar to that of karma, as discussed in The Wheel of Fortune (*see page 58*).

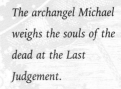

The archangel Michael weighs the souls of the dead at the Last Judgement.

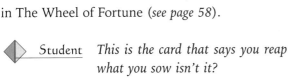 Student   *This is the card that says you reap what you sow isn't it?*

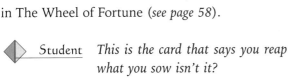 Juliet   Indeed. The idea of reaping what we have sown and taking responsibility for the consequences of our choices is a theme that is constantly repeated throughout the tarot images in many and various ways. Ultimately, it is one of life's most profound lessons. We each face choices and our lives are largely shaped according to how we make those choices. We all start out in different ways, as dictated by the families into which we are born, but from then on we start making our own choices as to how we wish to live our lives, and then have to abide by our decisions. Unfortunately, although we do not have the advantage of being able to see in advance what will happen with each choice we make, we nevertheless have to live with the consequences – whatever they are.

The image of Judgement essentially describes that process of having made decisions in the past (symbolized by the graves) and being faced with the consequences in the present (the appearance of the angel). We can then make decisions for the future based on that past experience and its results. For example, if we have spent a lifetime telling lies, we may reach a 'moment of truth' in which we are able to see where our lies have taken us. We then have a decision to make about whether we wish to continue lying. Perhaps we have not been found out and see no reason to end the deceptions. On the other hand, we might feel uneasy and trapped, and decide to seize the moment Judgement offers us to end the lies and continue life with a clean slate. It is our choice, and we alone must bear the consequences.

XX · L'ANGELO · THE ANGEL ·

The figure emerging from the sarcophagus in the Renaissance deck represents the risen Christ. In the top right-hand corner is the angel and in the top left is a phoenix, a symbol of rebirth and resurrection.

Creative Fire

The sight of the dead rising joyfully, as in the Morgan Greer deck (*see page 96*), or even respectfully, as in the Visconti (*left*) and Wirth (*opposite page*) decks, is a warming image, and this card has a close link with the element of Fire. Fire is a symbol of creativity, and can be regarded as a source of both warmth and light,

Two angels sound the trumpet blast, while a godly figure sits between them. Three figures rise up to greet the call. The man and woman are thought by some historians to represent Francesco Sforza and Bianca Maria Visconti, as they believe that the cards were commissioned to celebrate their marriage or anniversary.

but also of destruction. Its symbolic connections include a range of options: anger and punishment, love and passion, purification and transformation. Many tarot decks include on the Judgement card the image of a large cross emblazoned on a banner, which is a symbol of the reconciliation of opposites out of which spiritual progress can be made.

As a fiery card, Judgement could be linked with the stage in the alchemical operation called calcination, the part of the process that involved heating the primal matter until it was reduced to ash. Spiritually, this symbolized the purging of the self of discontent and replacing it with optimism and longing for a better course. The man and woman could also be identified as the King and Queen whose union has produced the Divine Child, or Philosopher's Stone. The blast of the trumpet heralds the moment at which the Great Work will finally come to its triumphant conclusion.

• EXERCISE •

Find a quiet place to sit where you know you will not be disturbed for an hour. Look at the Judgement card closely and consider the image carefully. Muse upon it at length. What immediately springs to mind in relation to it?

Try to trace the crucial events and decisions that have taken place in your life and that have led to your current situation. Now look at the series of smaller choices you have made over the past year, which have brought you to this point. In the light of experience consider which decisions you made that you are satisfied with and which you would not wish to repeat.

The more consciousness you have about the events that have shaped your life and the choices you have made, the greater your own personal power will be in the future.

The angel on the Wirth card calls the three figures to life. They may represent the three alchemical ingredients of Philosophic Sulphur, Philosophic Mercury and Salt – all that is necessary to perform the Great Work.

Triumphant completion
End of a cycle
Success and fulfilment

THE WORLD

The figure on the Wirth card is holding the two wands in one hand; one is red and the other blue, symbolizing the masculine and the feminine combined.

The mythic origins of The World card are not at all clear. This card generally shows a semi-naked figure carrying two wands and surrounded by a wreath. In each corner of the card the faces of a bull, a lion, an eagle and a man appear. The figure dancing in the centre of the wreath, whose sex is concealed by a sash, seems to represent the triumph of attainment rather than be an actual mythic figure or story.

Perfect Balance Achieved

The successful blend of opposites into a single perfection is depicted by the four elements, which are symbolized by placing the image of the heads of a bull, lion, eagle and man in each corner of the card and the dancing figure within the circle. They represent the four elements of Earth, Fire, Water and Air, respectively, as well as the fixed signs of the zodiac, which mark the seasons. The fixed signs are Taurus, Leo, Scorpio and Aquarius, which correspond to spring, summer, autumn and winter. The four corners also mark the four compass points, the four winds and the four evangelists of the Christian tradition: St Luke, St Mark, St Matthew and St John, whose names were evoked by children through the ages in bedtime prayers: 'Matthew, Mark, Luke and John, Bless the bed that I lie on.'

In Christian art, the ellipse is often used to symbolize ascent, and it can be seen in paintings of the Virgin Mary and of Christ ascending into heaven. Once perfection has been achieved, it has no place on this earth. A purple or red sash, the colours of wisdom and divinity, drapes the dancing figure so as to hide the gender. This figure is often thought to be hermaphrodite, a symbol of the union of male and female to achieve perfect harmony. The two wands illustrate the need to find balance between the opposites that The Fool has had to encounter on his journey. They can now be held in accord. The Fool's journey through the tarot has been a constant struggle to unify opposing forces and balance opposites, and the image of the dancer in the circle is a symbol of his success.

Reaching the Journey's End

The image of The World used in the Visconti deck (*below*) is untypical. Here two cherubs hold up a circle containing a magical, walled city. It is quite possible that the fairytale city is a symbol of the 'goal achieved', in which case it could be golden Jerusalem, said to be the earthly counterpart to the shining city of heaven, or the Arthurian Avalon or perhaps the classical Garden of Hesperides.

According to Arthurian legend, Avalon was the wonderful isle to which King Arthur was carried to be healed of his wounds. It was also the place where the blessed dead were taken and where, in some versions of the myth, Arthur still exists as an immortal. The name of Avalon has connections with the festivals of apples held at the autumn equinox. The Greek garden of Hesperides was also a paradise in which a tree grew that bore golden apples. One of Heracles' labours (*see page 60*) was to steal three of the golden apples, although Athene later arranged for their safe return. This happy place was inhabited by nymphs who personified the clouds made gold by the setting sun.

Whichever city is represented on this card, the goal symbolized by The World is the completion of the journey, the arrival of The Fool at the 'happy land'. In alchemical terms, it marks the culmination of the Great Work in the Philosopher's Stone.

Culmination of the Great Work

The image of The World in the tarot can be associated with the culmination of the Great Work of the alchemist. The passionate fusion of the King and Queen is symbolized by the androgynous figure in the centre of the circle. The Sun and Moon combine; gold and silver are balanced – the union of masculine and

Two cherubs in the Visconti deck hold up a globe containing a vision of paradise. The four elements are represented by the sea, land, air and stars around the miniature city.

Ouroboros, the dragon, feeds on its own tail (right). The colouring is part of the alchemical art. Green is the beginning of the Great Work; red is the goal of the Great Work.

The wreath in the Universal Waite deck is made up of laurel leaves, the symbol of success, and the red ribbons suggest achievement.

feminine gives birth to the Philosopher's Stone. In addition, the oval wreath symbolizes the ouroboros, the snake eating its own tail. The ouroboros represents the cyclical nature of the work, and the constant renewal of life. The four elements, as symbolized by the four creatures in each corner of The World card, combine to create the perfect fifth, the Quintessence (*see page 86*). In *The Tarot*, Richard Cavendish asserts that this card provides a mystical sense of being at one with nature, of being merged with the underlying unity of all life, bringing a conviction of immortality.

THE WORLD.

Student   *It sounds too good to be true! Does it mean you will live happily ever after if you pick this card?*

Juliet   No, sadly not! We are never destined to live in a constant state of happiness in this realm I am afraid! However, it is a great card, which suggests that a moment of completion has been reached and a new cycle is about to begin. As the wreath on The World card is egg-shaped or womb-like, the dancing figure can be seen to represent the foetus in the womb ready to be reborn again as The Fool. The procession of trumps ends with The World, which is both a joyful end and an exciting beginning combined in one. After all, the minute something is complete it loses its charm. For example, imagine you have been struggling for a very long time to paint a picture. At last it is finally finished to your satisfaction and then exhibited. At first you feel a sense of elation with the successful completion of your work, but that is usually quickly followed by new ideas that begin to form about the next painting you will do.

The arousal of such feelings are not only caused by the successful completion of a work of art. The same feelings arise with any project at all. The main point to remember is that once something is complete and nothing more can be added, it is time to move on. To take another analogy, if you are working for exams, or a university degree, say, it is a wonderful achievement to get the grades you want. However, once the moment of elation and joy at the success has passed, you arrive at the next stage, which would be to move on to a higher form of study or to find a job. And so The World brings you back full circle to The Fool.

• EXERCISE •

This last card in the Major Arcana shows a stage of completion. If you have been following the cards in sequence it will mean you have reached a completion of your own. How does it feel? What has the process meant to you? Take a note of how it feels to complete something. Does it feel a relief or a disappointment? Are you ready for the next stage? Think of the times in your life when you have completed tasks and recall the different feelings and emotions around the event. Make a note of them.

Now consider where you are personally in the procession of trumps. Use the image of The World card to make a final guided-imagery exercise. Follow the usual breathing techniques to calm your mind and prepare for meditation. Now allow your imagination free rein to wander around the picture and allow the image to speak. If you like, find a piece of music or a perfume with which to associate this final card.

The wreath on the Medieval Scapini card is made up of the fruits and flowers of the Earth, while the alchemical snake winds itself through the foliage.

CHAPTER TWO

THE MINOR ARCANA

This chapter explores some of the general themes that run through the four suits of the Minor Arcana. I explain the correlation between each of the court cards and the four elements of Earth, Air, Fire and Water, and the three astrological qualities – cardinal, fixed and mutable. The connection between each of the twelve signs of the zodiac and the Knight, Queen and King of each suit is also revealed. The chief characteristics of the zodiacal signs as they relate to the court cards are discussed, providing a deeper understanding of each of them. Finally, divinatory interpretations are offered for each of the Court cards. The numbered cards are not for-

Phœnix

gotten. The traditional meanings associated with each number from one to ten are provided, together with specific meanings associated with each number of each suit.

I have used the Waite deck to illustrate this chapter because the deck is well known and its imagery provides clear symbolism for the elements, making them easy to identify. The element of Water is obvious in the Suit of Cups with the predominant use of blue and the prevelance of water and fish motifs. The rich browns and greens that dominate the Suit of Pentacles, together with the motifs of grapes and flowers that adorn it, make it easy to connect this suit with the element of Earth. Salamanders and sunflowers, with their warm red and yellow hues make the Suit of Wands easy to identify with the element of Fire, while the steely grey tones and prevelance of motifs of birds and sky connect the Suit of Swords quite naturally with the element of Air.

THE FOUR SUITS

The four suits of the tarot – Cups, Wands, Swords and Pentacles – are the forerunners of the modern-day playing deck of Hearts, Clubs, Spades and Diamonds. Each suit is associated with one of the four astrological elements – Water, Fire, Air and Earth. On a practical level, the four elements represent everything you need to live; that is, water, warmth, oxygen and food. A consistent combination of all four are vital to sustain physical life. The element of Water is reflected in Cups, Fire in Wands, Air in Swords and Earth in Pentacles. The four cardinal virtues are also echoed in the four suits: Temperance in Cups, Strength in Wands, Justice in Swords and Prudence in Pentacles.

Each element is also associated with a function of the psyche, and to sustain a healthy psyche you need to keep the four elements in balance psychologically. The great Swiss psychologist Carl Gustav Jung conceived the scheme of psychological types. He believed that each personality is composed of four functions: feeling, intuition, thinking and sensation, which are associated with the elements as follows: feeling with Water, intuition with Fire, thinking with Air and sensation with Earth. He held that for each psychological type one of these functions predominates and therefore governs the way in which the person relates to the world. According to Jung, the psychological process of individuation involved in achieving a balance between the

four typologies would result in a perfect whole. This notion is reflected in the thinking of medieval alchemists, whose goal of alchemical gold is very close to the Jungian goal of psychological individuation.

Mythological Links

The emblems of the Minor Arcana are reflected in myth. In Greek myth, for example, the attributes of Hermes included: the cup of fortune, from which he would invite mortals to sip to change their fortune in love (Cups); the caduceus, his magical wand entwined by two snakes representing all opposites (Wands); the mighty sword given to him by his father, Zeus (Swords); the bag of coins that marked him as the god of merchants and thieves (Pentacles).

The four emblems can be found in Grail myth, too. The sacred objects found in the Grail Castle included the chalice (Cup) used by Jesus at the Last Supper as the Holy Grail itself; the lance of Longinus (Wand), used by the Roman soldier to pierce Christ's side as he hung from the cross, causing water and blood to flow in separate streams; King David's sword of the spirit (Sword); and the platter (Pentacle) from which the Last Supper was eaten.

Finally, each object is also associated with a Celtic deity: the Cup with the Cauldron of the Dagda, the nourishing All Father, whose magic cauldron could never be emptied (*see page 73*); the Wand with the special Spear of Lug, the wonderfully creative and versatile god whose nickname was 'many skilled'; the Sword with the mighty weapon of the Nuada, King of the Tuatha de Danaan, which was so powerful that no enemy could escape from it; and the Pentacle with the Stone of Fal, the enchanted coronation seat that would cry out when sat upon by the rightful King of Ireland.

Interpreting Each Card

In addition to the association of particular elements, virtues, temperaments and objects from myth with the four suits, the numbers of the cards also have symbolic meanings. The chart on the next two pages describes the traditional meanings of the numbers one to ten and provides specific interpretations for each card of each suit, combining the number influence with all the other associated meanings.

THE NUMBERS

Ace or One	Two	Three	Four	Five
The number of pure energy and undiluted source of power. One is the number that represents beginnings.	*The single energy of the Ace is split and marks a duality. Opposites form, resulting in the need for balance and harmony.*	*The number of growth and movement. It marks the completion of the first stage of a relationship, project or vision.*	*The number of reality, logic and reason. It represents solidity and stability.*	*The number of uncertainty, instability and of frequent changes and shifts. It is a difficult number in the tarot.*

THE SUIT OF CUPS

Ace of Cups	Two of Cups	Three of Cups	Four of Cups	Five of Cups
Powerful new beginnings in the realm of feelings and relationships. A period full of potential and possibilities regarding relationships or projects of a very personal nature.	*Balance in relationships; a time for cooperation in partnership; the beginning of a new love affair or platonic friendship; reconciliation and compromise.*	*A time of celebration and joy. Something that has been long awaited is welcomed: this could pertain to marriage, birth or the achievement of a long-held goal.*	*A time of boredom or frustration. There is an inability to make good use of the advantages one has; a tendency not to see what is positive, only what is not.*	*A period of change. A loss or regret over past actions: something remains positive in the situation and attention has to be paid not only to the difficulties but also the possibilities.*

THE SUIT OF WANDS

Ace of Wands	Two of Wands	Three of Wands	Four of Wands	Five of Wands
A powerful surge of imaginative and creative energy; inspiration and optimism for new projects and ideas.	*Ideas have been translated into action but there is still much to be done. High aims and the promise of success to be gained through strength; initiative can overcome obstacles.*	*The initial completion of an idea or project; a sense of satisfaction and accomplishment; efforts are rewarded yet more can still be done.*	*A time of relaxation, rest and reward after hard labour; energy has been well expended and the benefit is now reaped. A positive and productive card.*	*A time of frustration and delay; petty obstacles and irritations interfere but are short-lived. It is a time in which your wishes and reality clash.*

THE SUIT OF SWORDS

Ace of Swords	Two of Swords	Three of Swords	Four of Swords	Five of Swords
A new beginning, which offers great power and strength. Conflict may be necessary to force changes and seek new and better solutions.	*Fear of facing reality; the desire to avoid choices or decisions. A stalemate has been reached yet the balance must be upset to make positive change.*	*Quarrels, separations or difficulties in relationships; by cutting away the old, dead wood you make way for new shoots. Understanding the situation puts sorrow into perspective.*	*A time for repose and convalescence and recovery after hard work, tension and strain. A quiet time for meditation and relaxation is necessary.*	*Know your limits before making changes; certain obstacles exist that must be acknowledged and worked with before successful changes can be achieved.*

THE SUIT OF PENTACLES

Ace of Pentacles	Two of Pentacles	Three of Pentacles	Four of Pentacles	Five of Pentacles
Positive material indications, including good health and financial rewards. A good time for beginning a financial proposition or a business venture.	*Changes and movement in fortune. The need to be flexible in business and financial affairs, although there is harmony within the fluctuation.*	*A structure is finished and an initial completion of work has been achieved. Approval and recognition gained through hard work and sustained effort.*	*Fear of letting go or taking a risk can cause stagnation. There is a sense of being stuck, for without risk nothing can change or move.*	*Loss, which may be financial, emotional or spiritual – perhaps loss of faith. Difficulties in business or material matters; the need to pay close attention to detail.*

Six	Seven	Eight	Nine	Ten
The number of harmony and balance, and of warmth and security.	The number of wisdom, knowledge and expansion. It also represents reflection, individualism and mysticism.	The number of death, regeneration and new life. It is also the number of justice, practicalities and perseverence.	The number of resurrection and gathering things together before completion.	The number of completion before starting again with the Ace; the end of a phase or cycle.

Six of Cups	Seven of Cups	Eight of Cups	Nine of Cups	Ten of Cups
A time of nostalgia and happy memories: a long-held dream from childhood comes about; an old friend or lover from the past returns; seeds of the past bear fruit in the present.	Creativity and talent are plentiful yet so is confusion. Decisions must be made concerning creative and relationship matters, which is hard because there is so much choice.	A time to let go of old ways and find new expressions. The old ways of relating have passed and it is time to find new ones.	A time of emotional satisfaction and fulfilment. This is traditionally known as the 'wish' card, meaning that a profound longing or desire could be met.	A time of contentment and reward after hard effort. Good fortune as a result of hard effort.

Six of Wands	Seven of Wands	Eight of Wands	Nine of Wands	Ten of Wands
Success and public recognition is achieved. Promotion and prospects in the workplace auger well; promise of fulfilment in public life.	Stiff competition follows success; a time for perseverance and courage in order to win over any opposition and meet difficulties.	A time of action and excitement; a busy period in which much can be achieved. A time in which the prevailing circumstances help rather than hinder the pursuit of your goals.	Strength in reserve and the need for determination in the face of opposition or adversity. Travel, journeys and moves are likely.	Beware of ignoring physical limitations: there is a danger of becoming overburdened by not setting firm enough boundaries.

Six of Swords	Seven of Swords	Eight of Swords	Nine of Swords	Ten of Swords
Moving away from stress and difficulties towards a more satisfactory and peaceful situation. Release of tension and anxiety bringing a time of calm.	A time to use the mind carefully, tactfully and diplomatically rather than trying to achieve goals aggressively or by being overtly hostile.	The restrictions and limitations that this card imply are often self-imposed and remain because of fear and indecision. Positive action can change the status quo.	Fantasies and thoughts of impending doom are not realized; fears and doubts are much worse than the true situation.	A vision of truth and clarity of understanding make way for new understanding; disappointment and disillusion end false hopes and clear the decks for a new outlook.

Six of Pentacles	Seven of Pentacles	Eight of Pentacles	Nine of Pentacles	Ten of Pentacles
Generosity and kindness shown by friends or benefactors; financial aid or gifts. It may be that generosity or charity is required from you.	Pause during the development of business or enterprise during which a different avenue can be pursued; decisions that will be far-reaching must be taken.	New directions can be taken in your work or career; skills or talents can be mastered in order to take up a new job; a good time to embark upon a field of study or apprenticeship.	Material and financial security and contentment; gratification and satisfaction achieved through commitment and hard work.	Forming solid foundations for families or business; the purchase of property as a symbol of security or founding a tradition; the addition of stability and permanence to life.

THE COURT CARDS

The court cards act as a bridge between the Minor and Major Arcanas. They may refer to an event, a person entering the seeker's life, an aspect of the seeker's own personality or an aspect that the seeker needs to develop. With such a wide range of possibilities, interpreting the court cards can be difficult. The key is to be flexible and intuitive in your approach. It is also important to involve the seeker in the process – there is nothing the matter with asking which interpretation seems most pertinent to the person whose cards are being read. As always, in order to be confident when reading the tarot, it is vital to achieve a real understanding of the symbolism. Study the images on the cards and allow their meanings to unfold naturally. Avoid learning a set of key words and sticking to them rigidly.

Astrological Links

One way of understanding the court cards better is to consider both the elements and the astrological qualities with which the signs of the zodiac are associated. The three astrological qualities – cardinal, fixed and mutable – represent the three basic principles of life: something is born, lives and dies (or changes in order to be born again). So, car-

dinal signifies creation, fixed signifies preservation and mutable signifies destruction. In the tarot, the Kings are associated with the cardinal signs, which instigate action; the Queens are connected with the fixed signs, which preserve and contain; and the Knights are represented by the mutable signs, which change and dissolve.

The cardinal signs are characterized by outgoing, active, forceful and dynamic energy, which is expressed through the particular element with which the quality is connected and its corresponding suit. The four cardinal signs are Aries (Fire), Cancer (Water), Libra (Air) and Capricorn (Earth). The Kings in the tarot are associated with power, authority, action and accomplishment.

The energy of the fixed signs is expressed through consistency, reliability and patience. The Queens represent containment, receptivity and stability: they are able to nurture and bring to fruition that which the Kings create. The four fixed signs in astrology are Taurus (Earth), Leo (Fire), Scorpio (Water) and Aquarius (Air).

The mutable signs are characterized by energy that is flexible, volatile and adaptable. The Knights in the tarot are always seeking new goals and challenges; they are 'on the move' and always restless. The four mutable signs in astrology are Gemini (Air), Virgo (Earth), Sagittarius (Fire) and Pisces (Water).

The Pages

The Pages are not attributed any particular quality; rather they reflect the essence of the element to which their suit is connected. As Pages are traditionally associated with messengers or children, they represent the potential of their particular element.

• Page of Cups – *a gentle, loving person who offers friendship, or who brings news of a birth, a child or an idea. The fragile beginnings of a relationship.*

• Page of Wands – *inspiration in creative matters; an energetic influence in the form of an enthusiastic friend or a brilliant idea.*

• Page of Swords – *a new way of thinking starts. The mind can be put to positive or negative use: kind words and encouragement or malicious gossip.*

• Page of Pentacles – *perseverance and determination can eventually turn a skill or talent into a career or a way of life.*

THE KINGS

KING of CUPS.

The cardinal quality of this card suggests action and decision, which sometimes conflicts with the tenderness of the Water element.

The King of Cups

The King of Cups sits on a throne that stands in the sea, but unlike the Queen of Cups, who appears almost to melt into the water, he is separate from the sea. He holds his cup as though it were a symbol of power, unlike the Queen, who gazes at her cup tenderly. Around his neck hangs a golden fish, symbolizing ordered creativity, while another fish leaps in the background, symbolizing his need to push his spontaneous feelings to the back of his mind.

The King of Cups is often associated with the Church, law or the healing professions, such as medicine or counselling. He is instrumental in helping others to gain a good understanding of their own needs or to heal their physical or emotional wounds, although he may not always be successful in managing this for himself. It is as though he wants to understand his emotional world fully, yet at the same time is afraid of the challenge. Unlike the Queen of Cups, who dives willingly into the depths of her emotions, the King is more hesitant. The cardinal water sign of Cancer is connected with this card, and, while the realm of feelings is extremely important to Cancerians, they have a tendency to be wary of intimacy and find trusting others difficult.

• INTERPRETATION •

When this card appears in a reading it can mean that a person is about to enter your life who is full of good intentions and kindness but who is also rather wary emotionally. Alternatively, it may suggest that you feel inhibited or shy in relationships or perhaps are frightened by intimacy, although your desire to form close relationships makes you want to overcome this fear.

The King of Wands

The King of Wands sits forward restlessly on a throne decorated with the motifs of fiery lions and salamanders, the legendary creatures thought to inhabit flames. On the ground by his side a live salamander is positioned. He represents the cardinal Fire sign of Aries, the first sign of the zodiac.

The King of Wands is an energetic figure who is always ready for adventure, always able to come up with a fresh view on any subject and possesses a seemingly unquenchable optimism. He is blessed with a charm and wit that inspires those around him to move mountains. Those born under the sign of Aries have the knack of making other people excited about their projects and ideas and for this reason often excel in sales and marketing. Ariens are also known for their creative and artistic flair, which is common to all the Fire signs, who have the ability to 'see' what something will look like: for example, they can look at an empty room and visualize it fully decorated and furnished. The King of Wands is not knowingly manipulative or malicious, although those who buy into his schemes may be disappointed that he often loses interest in the project once the deal is done. He is an innovator, a creator and a leader – not a follower.

The King of Wands is sometimes known as the 'salesman', as he can inspire and enthuse others to join him or buy into his ideas.

• INTERPRETATION •

When the King of Wands appears in a reading he adds a creative spice to your life, whether through the appearance of a warm, generous, fiery friend, or through an increase of your own inspiration and creative energy. This card suggests that the time is now ripe for you to develop your creative skills, whether privately at home or with the help of a friend or teacher.

The King of Swords

The King of Swords is seated on a throne that appears to be raised high in the clouds. He wears a purple cloak – the colour of wisdom – yet his sword is tilted to the right, suggesting ambivalence: if it had been exactly vertical then it would represent pure wisdom. The King of Swords is connected with the cardinal Air sign of Libra and the two birds in the background symbolize the duality of this sign.

Librans are always able to see both sides of a situation and to weigh up one thing against another in order to reach a fair solution. Librans appreciate balance, order and harmony, and dislike injustice, inequality and uncivilized behaviour. The King of Swords is traditionally connected with justice and the law, he is a firm but fair authority figure. Air is the element connected with thinking and in many respects it is this function of man that presents the most difficulties. Unlike the animal kingdom, where instinct and desire rule and the weakest perish, humans are constantly considering questions of social justice and equality, and the ethics of war. The King of Swords represents the need to examine these complexities and at the same time to accept that no perfect solution exists and that some problems are insoluble.

The King of Swords stares straight ahead as though willing to confront and consider any issue head on.

• INTERPRETATION •

When the King of Swords appears in a reading it may be that an intellectual, questioning person is about to enter your life and kick-start you into examining your own way of thinking. It is also possible that you start this process on your own as new ideas gained from study or reading stimulate fresh ways of thinking about things.

יהוה

The King of Pentacles

The King of Pentacles sits comfortably on his throne in a robe decorated with rich purple grapes and bulls' heads, the bull being a symbol of potence and fertility. The vine leaves that surround him appear to merge into his robes as though he is at one with nature. The King of Pentacles is associated with the cardinal Earth sign of Capricorn.

Power, authority and status, which are often aligned with wealth, are all-important to Capricorns. All the cardinal signs like to see action and results, and the King of Pentacles likes to see an increase in material goods as a way of making life more enjoyable. The Earth signs all enjoy physical comforts and objects of beauty and the more money, luxury and beauty that can be obtained, the better. The King of Pentacles is not only interested in acquiring wealth to buy 'things', he also needs money to acquire status, a standing in the community, power and leadership, symbolized by the castle in the background. However, like the other Earth signs and suits, he is content once he has achieved his goals, and as long as he is able to maintain his position, he is satisfied. He is always prepared to put in every ounce of effort required to do this and does not shirk responsibility.

The King of Pentacles seems comfortable and contented with his achievements. He possesses the unique capacity to enjoy the fruits of his labours.

• INTERPRETATION •

When the King of Pentacles appears in a reading, someone who is at home with the material world or the world of business and finance may be about to enter your life, or you may commit yourself, through hard work and effort, to matters of this nature. The realm of the physical world will need attention when this card appears, and practical issues must be appropriately considered.

The Queen of Cups

The Queen of Cups is a dreamy, gentle-looking woman, who gazes intently at the elaborate cup with handles in the shape of winged angels. These suggest her link with the spiritual realm, while the symbolic emphasis on water – for example, the mermaids, shells and fish that decorate her throne – connect her to the world of feelings. Her blue and white cloak is reminiscent of the sea and the coloured pebbles represent the jewels of the ocean, which correlate with the richness and depth of the feelings.

The Queen of Cups is the queen of emotions. Her aim is to understand and experience the depth of her feeling nature, so relationships and the feelings of both her own and those of others are of the utmost interest to her. Scorpio is the sign of fixed Water, the element associated with volatile and unpredictable emotions, and Scorpios are well known for their passionate, intense natures. The fixed nature of Scorpio means that they are fiercely loyal to their loved ones, and show a deep interest and commitment to any person or cause close to their heart. The Queen of Cups is traditionally known as the Beloved One, as her emotional honesty and personal magnetism draw others to her.

The beauty and mystery of the Queen of Cups evokes intense fascination in others as the world she rules is so important and yet at the same time so secret.

• INTERPRETATION •

If this card appears in a reading, it may be that it is time for you to delve into the ocean of your own feelings, or that a person with the Queen of Cups' qualities will enter your life, alerting you to feelings you have been unaware of until now. It is a time for emotional honesty; feelings need your full attention. It may also suggest an interest in creative or artistic pursuits.

The Queen of Wands

The Queen of Wands sits confidently on a bright throne ablaze with golden sunflowers and lions, reflecting the fixed Fire sign of Leo. The lions that decorate her throne represent her power and authority in the world, while the black cat at her feet reveals her role as homemaker and queen of the hearth. The gold of her dress hints at the Sun, which rules Leo.

Leo is a fiery sign and the Queen of Wands has no shortage of the energy, vitality and enthusiasm characteristic of this sign. As a character, the Queen of Wands suggests the kind of person who is able to achieve a great deal. She represents the ability to pursue many activities at once: she manages to be successful in her chosen career, follow many artistic and creative pursuits, as well as have time for relationships and family life – quite a feat! The fixed quality helps her to create a container in which to combine friendship and love, symbolized by the sunflowers, with the other creative interests she passionately pursues. The Queen of Wands suggests a remarkable ability to achieve great success and fulfilment both personally and professionally, fuelled by her tireless energy and an endless supply of optimism and enthusiasm.

The Queen of Wands holds the wand of creative power in one hand and the flower symbolizing relationships in the other, demonstrating her ability to partake equally of both.

• INTERPRETATION •

When this card appears in a reading it may be that some of the verve and vibrant energy it symbolizes is needed in your life and must either be generated by you or introduced by someone you meet who has these qualities. It may be a time in which you need to take risks or broaden your horizons to encompass a wider view of the world.

QUEEN of SWORDS.

The emphasis on sky and creatures of the air give this card a cool aspect, but also emphasize the importance of a clear mind.

The Queen of Swords

The Queen of Swords is seated bolt upright on her stone throne, which is decorated with angels and butterflies, symbolizing the element of Air. Her cloak is made out of a cloudy sky and above her flies a single bird, a symbol of wisdom and intellect. She gives the impression of authority and dignity, although she does not appear totally comfortable.

The Queen of Swords is traditionally known as 'a woman who has suffered' with the implication that she has been hurt through love. Yet she is not embittered by the suffering, for in the process she has gained wisdom. Rachel Pollack points out that the tassel hanging from the Queen's left wrist – left being the side of wisdom – looks like a cut rope. She has used the sword of intellect to cut through the pain to gain understanding, and she opens her hand to welcome the experience. The astrological sign connected with the Queen of Swords is Aquarius, the fixed Air sign. This sign is connected with high ideals and Aquarians often hold lofty visions of how the world and humanity could be, and are just as often disappointed by the fact that man has clay feet. Aquarius is ruled by Uranus, the ancient sky god who buried his children because they were ugly.

• INTERPRETATION •

Air signs seek perfection, and, as relationships are never perfect, when this card comes up in a reading it may suggest disappointment in a relationship that has not lived up to high expectations. It may also indicate that a person who has high ideals is about to enter your life, or that you need to examine your own expectations and ideals.

The Queen of Pentacles

The Queen of Pentacles is seated in a flowering garden, a bower of roses framing the card. These, together with the apples and pears decorating her throne and the arm-rest shaped in the form of the head of a goat, symbolize this Queen's connection with the Earth and its riches. A rabbit in the corner represents fertility and sexuality. The Queen of Pentacles is connected with Taurus, the fixed Earth sign associated with nature and natural processes.

Those born under the sign of Taurus are said to be calm and patient, fond of material comforts and sensual pleasures, responding positively to the five senses. Taureans enjoy delicious food, fine music, pleasing perfumes and objects that are beautiful to see and touch. The Queen of Pentacles represents a practical, earthy approach to life, a fondness for nature and home or family life. She is generous in offering financial help or practical aid and is a loyal friend. The simple things in life are sufficient to satisfy her and she is not impatient nor ambitious to achieve more than the safety and comfort of herself and her loved ones. The Queen of Pentacles concentrates on the material side of life, nurturing herself and others physically by paying attention to the body's needs.

Seated outdoors, surrounded by nature's bounty, the Queen of Pentacles emphasizes the richness of the natural world.

• INTERPRETATION •

The appearance of this card in a reading may signal that a person who possesses the pragmatic qualities of the Queen of Pentacles is about to enter your life and influence you accordingly. Alternatively, it may mean that you should pay more attention to the body and material side of life, to your health and comfort.

KNIGHT of CUPS.

Like the chivalrous knights of King Arthur, the Knight of Cups seeks the reward of perfect love.

The Knight of Cups

The Knight of Cups belongs to the mutable element of Water and the astrological sign of Pisces. The Waite deck shows the Knight calmly riding a beautiful white horse through peaceful countryside. A river meanders through the landscape, symbolizing the element of Water. His armour is decorated with fish, the symbol of Pisces, and he holds the golden cup of love in his outstretched hand.

He is traditionally known as the lover, the one who proposes marriage or brings romance, and in this card his whole demeanour is certainly gentle and refined. His winged helmet and heels represent his spiritual aspirations, as the love he seeks is not purely physical. The astrological sign of Pisces is concerned with love, romance and high ideals. However, because of the mutable quality of this sign, there can be conflict, symbolized by the two fish swimming in different directions. There may be conflict between the head and the heart, or longing for the kind of romance or love that does not exist in the realm of human existence. All the Knights in the tarot, and the mutable signs in astrology, are on quests. The Knight of Cups is on a quest for love of both a physical and spiritual kind.

• INTERPRETATION •

The divinatory meaning of this card may be the arrival of a lover, or a love affair starting, or a need to develop a romantic or soulful aspect in yourself. The appearance of this card in a reading means that a desire to encounter love assumes a position of importance in your life. It may be the love of another person, in either a platonic or romantic relationship, or it may be the love of art or religion.

The Knight of Wands

The Knight of Wands is an energetic, optimistic-looking figure, belonging to the mutable element of Fire and the astrological sign of Sagittarius. Unlike the sedate mount of the Knight of Cups, the Knight of Wands seems to be having difficulty 'holding his horses', an apt reflection of the sign of Sagittarius, which is always in a hurry and always on a journey in search of adventure. He is riding through a land with a hot climate, symbolizing the element of Fire.

KNIGHT of WANDS.

The Knight of Wands' quest is for meaning and knowledge for its own sake. He is not interested in knowledge in order to gain power or authority over others nor to make himself important in the eyes of the world. He is keen to acquire knowledge because it fascinates him and stimulates his imagination. His tunic is covered with salamanders – a symbol of fire – not all of whose tails reach their mouths, suggesting that plans have been formed but not completed. This, too, is typical of Sagittarians, who are always having brilliant ideas and starting projects, but as soon as they are up and running feel that it is time to move on to something new. A few of the salamanders do form a closed circle, representing completion or achievement, but many more do not.

The Knight of Wands gallops across barren lands with great enthusiasm. The necessity of having a good imagination is hinted at in the image.

• INTERPRETATION •

The Knight of Wands brings excitement, enthusiasm and a love of life when it appears in the reading. It may mean that a fiery, energetic person is about to arrive in your life, or that the qualities of the card are those you need to acquire yourself, or that the time has come for a move – of residence, country or job. The Knight of Wands brings with him a great restlessness and longing for change.

The Knight of Swords leans forward, holding out his sword as though to meet new challenges as speedily as possible.

KNIGHT of SWORDS .

The Knight of Swords

The Knight of Swords is connected with the mutable element of Air and the astrological sign of Gemini. The Knight of Swords is on a quest for truth, logic and intellectual knowledge. He holds high his sword, symbol of the mind and truth, as his horse fairly flies over windswept terrain. Trees bend in the wind and storm clouds dash across the skies. The motifs of birds and butterflies, winged creatures of the air, decorate his tunic and harness.

He seems in a huge hurry, typical of Geminis, who are always on the move, keen to pick up all and any pieces of information, useful or otherwise. Geminis are often known as 'jack of all trades and master of none' because they are inclined to collect snippets of information on a wide variety of subjects, yet never stay long enough to become deeply knowledgeable about any one of them. The butterfly is often used to represent them because it flits from flower to flower, sipping nectar from each but never settling. Movement and change is the essence of both Gemini and the Knight of Swords.

• INTERPRETATION •

If this card appears in a reading, it indicates that sudden, swift changes are about to occur. These may be brought about by meeting someone or by developing new ideas and ways of thinking. Traditionally, the Knight of Swords is said to bring conflict, but this may simply be the result of the sudden change this card brings. Although such a change may feel disruptive, it is also likely to be absolutely necessary to prevent stagnation.

The Knight of Pentacles

KNIGHT of PENTACLES

The Knight of Pentacles is connected with the mutable element of Earth and the astrological sign of Virgo. He is the only one of the Knights whose horse is stationary, standing in a ploughed field as the Knight calmly holds up his pentacle. The earth on which the horse stands is potentially fertile as it is ploughed and ready for sowing. The Knight's tunic is a rich brown, the colour of the earth, and his only decoration is a sprig of oak leaf. The oak is a tree that takes a long time to reach maturity, yet when fully grown is strong and mighty and lives for many years.

The mutable quality of Earth is evident in the quiet, industrious efficiency typical of the astrological sign of Virgo. The Knight of Pentacles, like Virgo, symbolizes hard work and persistence, yet is also resourceful and highly discriminating, always seeking perfection in an earthy craft. Virgos are often successful in their work because they are prepared to pay the necessary attention to detail required when translating ideas into actuality.

The Knight of Pentacles represents the potential and the determination to turn dreams into reality through practical application.

◆ INTERPRETATION ◆

If this card appears in a reading it can mean that a person possessing the Knight of Pentacles' qualities – that is, kindness, a love of nature and animals, and reliability – is about to enter your life. Alternatively, it could mean that you need to develop some of these qualities in yourself, or that an issue in your own life can be resolved through the application of patience, persistence and perseverance. The Knight of Pentacles is calm and steady, sometimes even accused of being boring, but he brings results.

CHAPTER THREE

WORKING WITH THE CARDS

Part of the human condition is the desire to find out what the future holds for us, and many people turn to the tarot in the hope of its discovery. A poetic explanation for our unquench-able curiosity can be found in the myth of Pandora and Prometheus, who, according to the Greeks, created man. Prometheus angered Zeus by stealing divine fire from Olympus to give to man. The gods pun-ished man by creating woman in the form of Pandora, who was given the double-edged gift of curiosity. Prometheus feared that man was

too fragile a creature to be able to bear knowing in advance what torment lay before him in the shape of this woman, so he took away the gift of foresight he had originally given man and replaced it with hope. So now we find ourselves in the impossible position of being incurably curious about the future yet unable to see what will happen.

This chapter is devoted to developing your practical work with the tarot. In it I show you four different spreads and explain their uses. There is also a detailed case study using one of the more complex spreads. Finally, I provide various story-telling exercises that will enable you to enrich and deepen your intuitive connection with the cards and your ability to join their meanings together in a cohesive reading. Practise the exercises as fully as possible, and adapt them to suit yourself. The more you are able to enter into a dialogue with the images, the more natural and spontaneous your readings will become.

THE TAROT AS GUIDE

When you work with the cards are you expecting them to enable you to foretell the future? The older generation of writers on the tarot made a clear distinction between divination, of which they approved, and fortune-telling, of which they did not. Divination was considered to be a serious-minded effort to penetrate mystery by an enlightened few, whereas fortune-tellers could be found at fairgrounds. They allowed their palms to be crossed with silver in exchange for revealing changes in fortunes, rivals in love and journeys across water with tall, dark strangers.

Using the Tarot for Divination

Early serious writers, such as Papus (*The Tarot of the Bohemians*, 1892), A. E. Waite (*The Pictorial Key to the Tarot*, 1910) and Paul Foster Case (*The Tarot: A Key to the Wisdom of the Ages*, 1947), felt that fortune-telling was like casting proverbial pearls before swine, and Waite remarked that the use of tarot trumps for telling fortunes was the 'story of prolonged impertinence'. Papus patronizingly assumed that his female readers would be too feather-brained to appreciate the profound spiritual significance of the cards. He expected them to be interested only in fortune-telling, so adjusted and simplified his instructions accordingly. Paul Foster Case, on the other hand, believed that anyone using the tarot for telling fortunes would be spiritually crippled, declaring that the tarot should be used only for the solution of serious questions, whether for self or others.

So, what exactly is the art of divination and how do you practise it using the tarot cards? Divination is concerned with bringing to light some sort of mystery by using the deep archetypal images and symbolism of the cards as a springboard. Divining by using the tarot is like plotting an emotional or spiritual weather forecast. The cards can intimate the best times for planting and reaping, sowing and harvesting, but they will not be specific about the crop. For example, the Death card can reflect a time of endings, changes or transformation, but the card does not specify whether the endings are welcome or dreaded, whether they refer to business or relationships, whether they are physical or spiritual. It is up to the seeker to consider how the idea of endings relates to his personal situation, thereby gaining a deeper understanding of his own unique circumstances.

When doing a reading, you should consider the image of each card that is drawn in the light of the seeker's position. The energy of The Fool, for example, will shine through completely differently in the life of a twenty-year-old to that of a sixty-year-old. The Fool's energy does not in itself change but the interpretation of that energy will be different for someone who is near the beginning of their life to someone who is approaching the end.

How to Read the Cards

Most tarot practitioners today would agree that it is not sufficient to learn the meanings ascribed to a particular card off by heart, lay them out in a particular format and then read them off by rote. In order to truly divine the meanings of the cards, there must be insight and intuition, which involves acquiring knowledge without necessarily knowing how it has been gained, consciously or unconsciously. This knowledge enters the conscious mind directly from an unknown source via the world of archetypal images found on the tarot cards, and is not limited to knowledge about the future; it can also reflect the past or present. The more you work with the cards, the greater will be your understanding. When doing a reading, try to think of yourself as a mediator between the archetypal images of the tarot and the seeker.

This kind of insightful knowledge can be enormously helpful to the seeker if their intentions are serious and thoughtful. Like the alchemists of old, for whom finding actual gold was secondary to the wisdom uncovered in the search, the seeker can use the tarot to uncover and understand more of the inner soul or unconscious mind. The more we know, the more choices we can make consciously. 'Knowledge is power', so the more we know about ourselves and our inner worlds, the more we can make good conscious choices and so direct our own destiny. The tarot can help in this process by guiding and illuminating the search but it will not (and perhaps we should not ask it to) tell us what we should do in a particular circumstance or what will happen in our lives. It is said that a good guide makes a bad master; the tarot should be used as a good guide.

CHOOSING A SPREAD

When doing a reading, you need first to decide which of the many different types of spread you will use and whether you will use the whole deck, or select cards only from the Major or Minor Arcana. This is largely a matter of personal choice and taste, although some spreads are more appropriate than others in certain cases. Experiment with different spreads to work out which you like best.

Using the Celtic Cross Spread

One of the best known spreads is the Celtic Cross, which is ideal for beginners because the position of each card has a clear meaning. It uses ten cards. For this reading you can use the whole deck or the Minor Arcana on its own if you prefer. The Minor Arcana conveys the

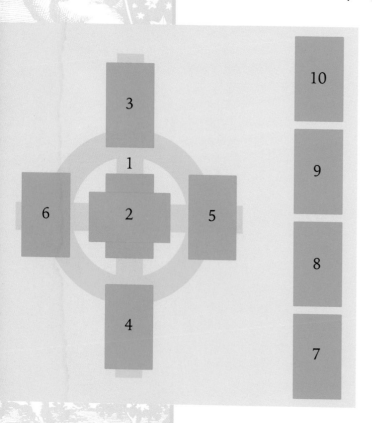

- 1. First position – *What is Present*

- 2. Second position – *What Crosses You, or what is difficult, or what frustrates you*

- 3. Third position – *What Crowns You, or what is uppermost in your mind*

- 4. Fourth position – *What is Beneath You, or what is moving out of your life*

- 5. Fifth position – *What is Behind You, or what happened in the recent past*

- 6. Sixth position – *What is Before You, or what will happen in the immediate future*

- 7. Seventh position – *Where You Will Find Yourself, or your position in the near future*

- 8. Eighth position – *How Others See You, which may not be how you view yourself*

- 9. Ninth position – *Your Hopes and Fears*

- 10. Tenth position – *The Outcome, giving the conclusion of the reading*

רְוֹחָה

everyday details of the seeker's life, while the Major Arcana provides an overview of the psychological dimension. I personally like to do the Celtic Cross with the Minor Arcana followed by the Star spread using the Major Arcana, to give a balance between the two. However, it is equally valid to use a mixed deck for both readings. It is really a matter for personal choice – there is no right or wrong way.

Using the Star Spread

The Star spread uses seven cards. It does not need to be read in terms of past, present and future. What is important is that it is read in terms of the position of each card. The cards can be paired off and read together or contrasted and seen in opposition to one another, whichever seems more appropriate to the various combinations.

- 1. First position – *The Root of the Matter, or what is the background for the present*

- 2. Second position – *Emotions and Feelings*

- 3. Third position – *Thinking Process and Career Matters*

- 4. Fourth position – *The Heart of the Matter, or the crux of the matter around which the other cards revolve*

- 5. Fifth position – *That which Arises from the Unconscious, or things emerging without your being sure why or where they came from*

- 6. Sixth position – *Conscious Desires, or the things in life you know you want*

- 7. Seventh position – *The Top of the Matter, or the outcome for the reading*

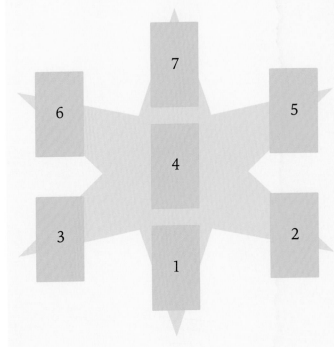

Using the Horseshoe Spread

The Horseshoe spread is ideal if you need to ask a specific question. It uses five cards and lends itself well to a mixed deck of both the Major and Minor Arcanas. This spread is short and relatively easy to interpret, so it can be a useful addition to one or two of the other spreads, acting as a summary. I often use the Horseshoe spread in this way, after having completed readings using the Celtic Cross spread followed by the Star spread.

If you wish, you can build on a reading using the Horseshoe spread by placing additional cards in each of the five positions. This will provide an extra layer or layers of information regarding the subject of each position, to create a more in-depth reading.

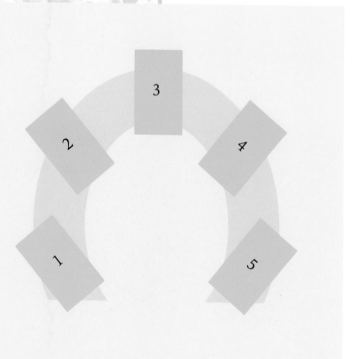

- 1. First position – *The Current Position in which you find yourself*

- 2. Second position – *What You Expect out of life at the moment*

- 3. Third position – *What You Do Not Expect, a surprise of some sort*

- 4. Fourth position – *The Immediate Future, what is in store in the near future*

- 5. Fifth position – *The Longer-Term Future, what the seeker can expect to happen over the coming year*

רחית

Using the Planetary Spread

The Planetary spread, an example of the use of which follows on the next page, is a good spread to use for a general reading. It is particularly popular with those who are confident in astrology as it combines the tarot and astrology very effectively.

In astrology, the Moon represents the emotional, feeling side of life; Mercury represents the mind, communication and adaptation; Venus represents love and beauty; the Sun symbolizes the outstanding characteristics of a person and what they seek to become; Mars is connected with the god of war, and the desire to compete and win; Jupiter is the king of gods, expansive and bountiful, bringing ideas and opportunities; Saturn is the planet of hard work, patience, perseverence and difficulties.

- 1. First position – *The place of the Moon. This position refers to home life and environment.*

- 2. Second position – *The place of Mercury. This position is concerned with business or career matters.*

- 3. Third position – *The place of Venus. This position is connected with relationships and love life.*

- 4. Fourth position – *The place of the Sun. This position is concerned with fame or achievement.*

- 5. Fifth position – *The place of Mars. This position describes where difficulties may lie.*

- 6. Sixth position – *The place of Jupiter. This position is connected with matters of expansion and gain.*

- 7. Seventh position – *The place of Saturn. This position is concerned with restriction and difficulty.*

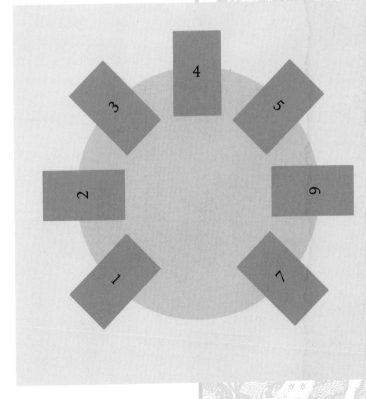

CASE STUDY

Ten of Swords

Ten of Pentacles

Mandy, a nineteen-year-old girl, came to see me because she was having difficulty deciding on the direction she should take. Should she continue with higher education or start working straight away? For this reading I used the whole deck. Seven cards were individually selected from the deck, which was spread out face down. I chose the Planetary spread because it gives specific information in rather a general way, which seemed appropriate in this case.

POSITION 1 – PLACE OF THE MOON
Home Life • Ten of Swords

Juliet It seems that you have been having a tough time at home just recently as the Ten of Swords is a card that indicates the end of a struggle or time of difficulty.

Mandy *That's right. Things have been quite stressful as I've been having lots of arguments with my mother about my future plans. I'm leaving next week to work in the United States where I have a placement in an advertising agency for about three months.*

Juliet The Ten of Swords describes the end of a particular phase and leaving home is undoubtedly a big step, marking the close of childhood. It is a bittersweet sort of card because, although it points to stress and difficulties, it also marks the turning point away from strife.

POSITION 2 – PLACE OF MERCURY
Work Life • Ten of Pentacles

Juliet The Ten of Pentacles is an earthy card, which symbolizes a successful conclusion to a project or piece of work. Its presence in the reading suggests that whatever you do in your work you will need to be practical and must appear to be useful. Mercury is the planet of the mind and is therefore flexible and versatile. However, combined with the earthiness of the Ten of Pentacles it means that thoughts and ideas must be translated into some sort of concrete reality.

Mandy *Would this be referring to my new work in the advertising agency in America?*

Juliet It would seem so as this spread refers to the fairly immediate future. I think what it is saying is that, in order to make an impression in this job, and in order to make significant progress, you must do more than just observe and learn from others, you must also be practically helpful, available and skilful.

POSITION 3 – PLACE OF VENUS
Love Life • The Moon

Juliet The Moon in the Place of Venus suggests that your feelings are going through a fairly uncertain phase just now. The Moon is a card of mood swings and lack of clear direction, so it would seem that your relationships with those close to you are in a somewhat confused state at the moment.

The Moon

Mandy *That's quite true! I have been seeing someone called James for several months and for a while it was ideal and we were very close. But then he had to go away and now that he is back things are different. I just don't know what is going on. He seems changed in himself, and I don't know what to think or feel any more. In fact, I feel pretty unsure about a lot of things in my life at the moment and my relationship with James is just one of them.*

Juliet When The Moon shows up in a reading it strongly suggests that no direct action should be taken as it marks a phase of uncertainty and lack of clarity, which is quite confusing. During such a phase it is not a good idea to try to force an outcome. Things will gradually become clear in the same slow way that the darkness of night eventually fades into the light of day. Your relationships are changing in lots of ways. As you enter this new phase of

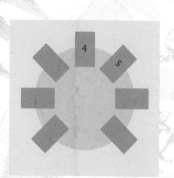

adult life, leaving home, loosening ties with your parents and becoming independent, you will find that the way you feel about many relationships will change. It is right that it should be this way; although it may not always be comfortable or easy, the occurrence of changing relationships is both healthy and inevitable.

◈ Mandy   *I can see what you are saying, and it is not very easy right now! But it is helpful to know that I should not be trying to make decisions when I just don't know what to do, even though everyone keeps telling me to decide things.*

◈ Juliet   For the moment it seems that waiting is all you can do. I know it is easy to say but very frustrating to do.

POSITION 4 – PLACE OF THE SUN
Position of Achievement • King of Cups

◈ Juliet   The King of Cups in the position of achievement seems to suggest that through understanding your feelings – represented by the watery Cups – you can move things along a great deal. The Kings stand for action which, in the case of Cups, suggests that your own feelings can be instrumental in creating change around you. It could also mean that someone is about to enter your life who embodies the qualities of the King of Cups: sympathetic, concerned with emotions, keen to form intimate relationships, yet who is also sensitive to, and afraid of, getting hurt. If this is a person, it is likely that he or she (it does not mean that it will be a man because it is a King) will make a significant impact on your life.

POSITION 5 – PLACE OF MARS
Position of Difficulty • The Hierophant

◈ Juliet   Some cards are hard to connect when they are placed in certain positions, and The Hierophant placed in the position of difficulty falls into this category! Bearing in mind your current situation, age and circumstances, a card like The Hierophant

King of Cups

The Hierophant

might feel almost inappropriate. After all, The Hierophant is connected with discovering one's own spiritual and philosophical position in life, and is about asking 'big' questions, which does not mesh well with being busy trying to choose a career direction and deciding on a course of study. However, The Hierophant is present in the reading, suggesting that, like it or not, whatever decisions you make must be grounded in a sense of deep meaning or purpose; it would be hard for you to take a direction that seems shallow to you.

Mandy *I think that is right. I do have lots of questions about 'the meaning of life' and my religious and spiritual beliefs have caused some conflict with my family. It is very important for me to have what I see as a 'spiritual' outlook, although my friends mostly do not share this, so I do feel quite alone with my thoughts.*

POSITION 6 – PLACE OF JUPITER
Position of Expansion • Eight of Wands

Juliet The Eight of Wands is a card of positive activity, which fits well in the position of Jupiter, the astrological planet that symbolizes expansiveness and beneficence. It indicates that life is opening up in opportunity and potential, which is hopeful in respect of your forthcoming travel plans. New ideas and experiences are beginning to reveal themselves to you, and it will prove an exciting and adventurous time, which you should certainly try to take advantage of.

Eight of Wands

POSITION 7 – PLACE OF SATURN
Position of Restriction • Seven of Pentacles

Juliet The Seven of Pentacles in the position of Saturn, the planet of limits and restrictions, shows that a serious choice is going to present itself. Of course, the difficulty about choice is that something has to be given up in favour of something else. In your case, it may be referring to the choice you have to make between taking a university position or going straight out to work. Obviously,

Seven of Pentacles

135

you have to decide which route you want to pursue but as the Moon is in the reading it may be best to leave this decision for a few months. Whenever the Moon's influence prevails it suggests that it may be premature to expect yourself to make a decision at the moment.

◇ *Mandy*　*Do you mean I can wait a bit before I decide definitely what to do about my university place?*

◇ *Juliet*　*I would say so.*

◇ *Mandy*　*What a relief! I really don't feel ready to decide yet but my mother has been on at me for ages to make up my mind. That is why she suggested I come for a reading. I am pleased I don't have to, but I am sure she won't be happy at all! I think she wanted you to tell me what to do.*

Conclusion

What seemed most important for Mandy was to have the time and space in which to consider her position before making a decision, and certainly the cards that she chose felt 'right' to her. The card that made the greatest impression on her was The Moon, as it described perfectly her mood swings and her feelings of confusion and doubt. She had felt caught between her own sense of not being in a position to make a decision about her future and the desire of her parents and 'society' for her to put their minds at ease by choosing a definite path. The reading gave her permission to listen to the part of her that needed more time to reflect and experience life before making a commitment.

STORY-TELLING EXERCISES

There is, of course, no easy solution to tapping into the deeper levels of meaning when doing readings, either for yourself or for others. Practice and experience is the only answer. There are, however, specific exercises that you can do to enhance and enrich your relationship with your cards. In the section on the Major Arcana I have suggested particular exercises to do with each card that will help you connect more fully with them. It would be useful to make similar connections with the Court cards, relating to the characteristics of each image. It would also be helpful to discover which characters you like, dislike, identify with and feel repelled by.

In this section I have outlined some more general story-telling exercises, which I hope will prove helpful in showing you how to respond intuitively to the cards. I strongly urge you to carry out all the exercises as fully as possible, as well as to expand and adapt them to suit you personally. The more you are able to enter into a dialogue or form a relationship with the images on each card, the more natural and spontaneous your readings will become. The only discipline required of you is to suspend rational thought and allow yourself to enter into the world of imagination as freely as you can.

Telling Your Life Story

Italo Calvino has written an ingenious and beautiful book called *The Castle of Crossed Destinies*, in which a group of strangers meet in an inn deep in a forest. Their power of speech is mysteriously taken away from them but one of them has a deck of tarot cards and they use the images on the cards to tell each other their life stories.

Using the cards like this can be a way of familiarizing yourself with your deck and increasing your confidence when interpreting the cards. Experiment with this method, either on your own or with a friend, using any number of cards. Choose images that you feel best illustrate a particular period in your life: events, important people, aspects of yourself and your feelings. If working with someone else, ask them to look at the cards to see if they can understand what you are trying to say through your choice of images. Then explain your choice.

We experimented with this method in a teaching group. We took it in turns to select five cards as a way of introducing ourselves. The first person to introduce himself was a middle-aged man, who chose the Three of Cups, the Ace of Pentacles, The Tower, the Eight of Pentacles and The Fool. The group had fun trying to interpret his story before the man gave his explanation.

He had been married (Three of Cups) and had made a lot of money (Ace of Pentacles), which had taken him away from his home and marriage. The marriage had eventually collapsed (The Tower) under the strain. At this point he felt as though his world had caved in on him, and his once beloved business suddenly lost its relevance. In response, he sold his business and moved away. The sale of his business provided him with enough of an income to pursue a new training (Eight of Pentacles) in alternative medicine. Now, several years later, he had finished his training and was qualified. He said he felt like The Fool (his final card) at the very beginning of a new cycle, the prospect of which was both exciting and frightening.

KEY

1. *Three of Cups*
2. *Ace of Pentacles*
3. *The Tower*
4. *Eight of Pentacles*
5. *The Fool*

KEY

1. *King of Pentacles*
2. *Six of Cups*
3. *Knight of Cups*
4. *Nine of Swords*
5. *Six of Swords*
6. *Knight of Wands*
7. *Ten of Cups*

Next, a young woman told her story. She said she was from a wealthy background (King of Pentacles) and had had a very happy childhood (Six of Cups). In her early twenties she had met a charming, handsome young man (Knight of Cups) with whom she had fallen madly in love. She assumed that they would live happily ever after. Consequently, she was extremely shocked when her lover left her for one of her close friends. It was the darkest time she had ever experienced (Nine of Swords) and it took her a long time to recover. To help manage this she went to live in another country (Six of Swords) where she met another man (Knight of Wands). She decided to stay with him in the new country and to make it her home. They are now married with a child (Ten of Cups), and she feels very contented.

The group felt that this exercise had been very useful because everyone had been able to offer an opinion on the images in question. It proved satisfactory as a learning experience, too, because the aim was to tease out a story rather than to be clever about reading future events as many people feel they should be when consulting the tarot.

Creating an Instant Story

Another way of expanding your personal experience with the cards is to make up your own stories, using the images on the cards as a springboard for your imagination. Turn over one card at a time and respond immediately and spontaneously to each image, creating a story as you go. I asked a child to make up an instant story in this way, using five cards. I wanted to let the images speak for themselves, completely unhampered by any kind of 'interpretation' of the meaning associated with each card. This was the child's instant response to the pictures as each card was revealed.

A CHILD'S OWN FAIRY TALE

1. Three of Wands: *'Once upon a time a man stood looking out for his son to come back from his travels.'*

2. High Priestess: *'The man was worried because his son was not home yet, so he went to visit the goddess of hope.'*

3. Two of Wands: *'The goddess told him to consult the wise man who lived in the rose lily castle.'*

4. Nine of Pentacles: *'As he was travelling he came to a lovely garden where he met a beautiful woman who loved birds. She told him to go home and wait patiently and that his son would soon return.'*

5. Four of Wands: *'The man was so impressed with the woman's kind words that he took her back to his castle. The son soon returned home and married the beautiful woman and they all lived happily ever after.'*

Using the tarot cards to tell a story can also be done by a group of people. One member of the group picks a card at random and starts telling a story, using the image as a starting point. Each of the other group members in turn picks a card at random and continues the story. The object of this exercise is to let your imagination run wild within the confines of the image on the card you have picked. This opens up your creativity in a completely new way.

There is no right or wrong answer when using the tarot to tell stories. This exercise is intended solely to encourage you to think in a new and different way, so do not consciously try to remember the divinatory meanings of the cards as you respond to the images. Let your instinct, or intuition, take over; allow your subconscious to speak. The results can range from the really creative to the quite bizarre, but the result is not important; it is the process that matters.

Index

Page numbers appearing in italics refer to illustrations.

Acknowledgments

AUTHOR'S ACKNOWLEDGEMENTS
Thank you to all at Eddison Sadd, to Jane Laing for all her hard work and, as ever, to Barbara Levy.

EDDISON • SADD EDITIONS
Illustrations from Visconti-Sforza Tarot reproduced by permission of U.S. Games Systems, Inc., Stamford, CT 06902 USA, Copyright © 1975 by U.S. Games Systems, Inc. Further reproduction prohibited.

Illustrations from Oswald Wirth Tarot reproduced by permission of U.S. Games Systems, Inc., Stamford, CT 06902 USA, Copyright © 1976 by U.S. Games Systems, Inc. Further reproduction prohibited.

Illustrations from Medieval Scapini Tarot reproduced by permission of U.S.

Games Systems, Inc., Stamford, CT 06902 USA, Copyright © 1985 by U.S. Games Systems, Inc. Further reproduction prohibited.

Illustrations from Universal Waite Tarot reproduced by permission of U.S. Games Systems, Inc., Stamford, CT 06902 USA, Copyright © 1990 by U.S. Games Systems, Inc. Further reproduction prohibited.

Illustrations from Morgan-Greer Tarot reproduced by permission of U.S. Games Systems, Inc., Stamford, CT 06902 USA, Copyright © 1993 by U.S. Games Systems, Inc. Further reproduction prohibited.

Illustrations from Renaissance Tarot reproduced by permission of U.S. Games Systems, Inc., Stamford, CT 06902 USA, Copyright © 1997 by U.S. Games Systems, Inc. Further reproduction prohibited.

Illustrations reproduced from The Mythic Tarot by permission of Eddison Sadd Editions Ltd. Copyright © Tricia Newell 1986. Published by Rider (UK), Fireside (US), Stoddart (Can) and Simon & Schuster (ANZ). Further reproduction prohibited.

Illustrations from The Arthurian Tarot by permission of Miranda Gray and John and Caitlín Matthews. Copyright © Miranda Gray 1990. The deck is published by HarperCollins Publishers, London (UK). Further reproduction prohibited. Visit the Matthews' website at www.Hallowquest.org.uk

EDITORIAL DIRECTOR ....*Ian Jackson*
EDITORS ....*Sophie Bevan, Jane Laing*
PROOFREADER ....*Ann Kay*
INDEXER ....*Helen Smith*
ART DIRECTOR ....*Elaine Partington*
SENIOR ART EDITOR..........*Pritty Ramjee*
PRODUCTION ....*Karyn Claridge, Charles James*